Fire in Forgotten, a fictional novel by Hope Kelley

Copyright 2020 by Hope Kelley

Cover Photo of South Texas Vaquero,
Samuel Torres, Jr.
Laura Canales, Photographer
Cover Design Illustration by
Hope Kelley

Hope Kelley Book Publishing

www.HopeKelleyBookPublishing.com

publish@HopeKelley.com

800.806.6240

Printed in the United States of America

Fire in Forgotten

by

Hope Kelley

Fire in Forgotten

"This novel has been a work in writing for many years. Putting it away for safe keeping, and years later, dusting it off... and writing and rewriting a little more...

It is lovingly dedicated to my families. The family with whom I grew up... most are no longer on this earth... and to the family with whom I now share my life. You are all my everything. Some of you... I greatly miss to this day. I love you all.

I also dedicate this book to my hometown. Whether you choose to stay or go, it always feels like home."

~~ Hope Kelley

FOREWORD

I have been fortunate to collaborate with Hope Kelley in my own writings and she is a remarkable Author and Publisher. Hope Kelley's passion for everything she does personifies her very being, and I am honored beyond words to write her Foreword for this book.

As the author of *Fire in Forgotten*, Hope Kelley is spectacular. The story is captivating from start to finish. It is riveting and filled with anticipation and surprise. It is believable and magnificent. I could not put it down. This book is a must-read and it would make for an amazing movie. You will love it!

~~ Lupita Almaraz Aguilar,
Author, *If The Hat Fits* and *Someone Is You*
Attorney at Law

PROLOGUE

In the late 1800's and into the twentieth century, many farmers and ranchers in Texas lost their homes and lands to the most powerful landowner. Families were threatened, burned from their homes, and in some instances, killed for the small piece of land they owned. Generations of families were lost along with their lands and heritage.

Fire in Forgotten is a western novel which spans decades, with the story beginning in 1928. This is the tale of two men, Henry Champion and George Baker, who feud their entire lives over a tragedy they witnessed as young boys. It is an unforgettable story of evil and hatred, paralleling a story of devotion, love, and undeniable passion.

I hope you enjoy reading this novel as much as I enjoyed writing it!

~~ Hope Kelley

CHAPTER 1
1928

The moon is bright in the late-night sky. It is an eerily quiet summer evening in the hill country, except for the sounds of the rhythmic hooting of owls and the chirping of cicadas. The tranquility is suddenly broken by four riders on horseback silhouetted against the horizon as they gallop over a rise on a hill. In the semi-darkness of night, their faces are unrecognizable, and seem ghostly with only the bluish light of the full moon reflected upon their faces. The men ride with purpose, and with destination in mind as they gallop over the countryside.

The riders approach an old cabin that has been there for the past fifty years. They quickly prepare fire torches and begin lobbing them at the old cabin as they ride by. They watch cheerfully as the rotting cabin easily catches fire. The old wood burns like kindle as the small structure begins to fall apart. An old man runs out of his long-time home with rifle in hand to defend his homestead. He is quickly shot down by one of the riders. The men laugh and gallop away as the cabin is now fully engulfed in flames.

The men ride away leaving the devastation behind. They travel for a few miles and come upon a small ranch house. They get busy lighting torches and throwing them into the home. The house quickly catches fire. The piercing sounds of a woman and children screaming come from inside. A man runs outside and is grabbed by two of the horsemen as another rider quickly shoots him down. The mother and her six little girls run out of the burning home in time to witness their father being shot before them.

With the full moon and the light from their home ablaze, the girls are able to get a good look at the horsemen before they ride away. The little girls cry as their father lies dead in the dirt and their home burns to the ground. The devastated mother takes them to the barn to harness a horse and wagon. The eight and nine-year-old girls help their mother lift the body of their father into the wagon. They all climb on board and sadly leave their home never to return. The echoes of the children's crying burn into the landscape forever.

It is a peaceful morning in the hill country as the sun rises and embraces a new day. A twelve-year-old boy is out early hunting in the brush. George Baker's eyes and ears are alert and listening. George spots a jack rabbit six yards away. He hears the noise of the rabbit rustle in the bushes as the rabbit searches for cover. George stands and takes aim. The jack rabbit's ears perk up. George is standing still and as quiet as he can. He raises his gun to take aim. It is plain the jack rabbit does not stand a chance if young George can shoot at all. He steadies his weapon. The cute little creature sees George. The jack rabbit and George gaze at one another for a long moment. George smiles at the cute little creature, its nose twitching and its big eyes staring at him.

It seems the rabbit acknowledges George's smile and friendliness and sits down but keeps a watchful eye. George is grinning as he shakes his head and has a change of heart about killing the endearing little animal.

"Sorry, Mom," tender hearted George mutters to himself. "You should send my older brother to fetch dinner."

As he lowers his rifle, he hears a woman scream in the distance. George freezes where he stands as the screaming continues. Back at George's farmhouse a devasting scene is developing. George's father, Patrick Baker, stands before the same four merciless riders. A young boy on a horse, around 12 years of age named Henry, accompanies the men this time. Henry's grandfather, John Champion, is clearly the leader of the gang.

John is a strong hard-looking man in his mid-sixties. His hair is graying, and his face features a thick moustache.   There is evil in his aging, strong eyes, and behind his formidable features, there is pleasure as he watches the fear in Patrick Baker's face. Patrick's family stands behind him. His wife of almost twenty years, Emma, his three daughters, and his eldest son stand huddled in fear as Patrick faces John Champion. As far as Patrick Baker knows, his other son, George, is out hunting for the family's dinner. He is praying George does not return soon. John Champion sits astride his horse and looks down on Patrick Baker.

Back in the brush, young George Baker crouches as he approaches his family's home. He hears the screams of his mother and sisters as the scene comes into his view. His sisters run away as George watches in horror as they are all shot in the back by Orlando and Martin, John's men. His home is now completely ablaze, and his mother is dragged to the river. George sees the fear in his mother's eyes as she struggles to get free, only to be forced down into the river by Martin. As his older brother tries to defend his father, he suffers the same fate as his sisters. John Champion and his men continue the destruction as George cries silently while hiding in the brush observing the devastation.

Frank Champion sits on his horse and watches with sadness but does nothing as his father and his men murder the innocent family. Frank is John's son and young Henry's father. He hates his father but fears him even more. He knows his father will kill him if he stands up to him. He worries about his son, Henry, growing up under his grandfather's influence. As all of this is happening, Frank decides he will take Henry and leave town tomorrow. He has wanted to leave many times, and he promises himself he will never return to Forgotten.

Hiding in the brush, George's eyes are now filled with tears, as they flow like a waterfall down his young and trembling face. He is helpless as he continues to watch the horror of his family's demise.

"Fine piece of dirt you got here, Patrick," John Champion says to Patrick Baker standing on the ground below him. "You've always known it would be mine one day."

"You're gonna rot in hell for this, Champion," responds Patrick, the pain and grief showing on his face, his eyes now clouded by fear and sorrow.

"Maybe," says John. "But you ain't gonna be around to see it."

With that remark, Patrick Baker turns and runs. John Champion draws his six-shooter and shoots Patrick Baker in the back. Baker falls lifeless to the dirt. Orlando and Martin snicker, and young George Baker sees his contemporary, young Henry Champion, observing the entire scene. George gasps for breath, at just witnessing his family's murders, as emotions fill his lungs.

"Grandpa, I don't see George nowhere," says young Henry.

"It don't matter, Henry. He wouldn't dare stay around here," mutters John Champion.

"Clean up this mess," says John Champion to his men.

"You're not going to get away with this, Father," states Frank Champion. "You're eventually going to pay for it all."

"You think so, son?" John says to Frank. "What are you going to do about it? Snitch on me to that idiot money-grubbing sheriff that runs Forgotten?" John Champion laughs out loud.

Yelling at his grandson he says, "Let's go, Henry."

Young Henry has a concerned and sad look as he turns his horse to follow his grandfather. It is obvious that Frank has been bullied and intimidated by his father his entire life. Henry does not like it but he is powerless to do anything about it. Henry knows his grandfather's wishes must be honored. He knows his grandfather is in charge. Frank looks around the farmhouse with sadness. He will not allow his son to be a part of his father's death and destruction. He rides away as the farmhouse on fire blazes against the morning sky.

"This has to stop," Frank mutters to himself.

Young George is still hiding in the brush and sobbing as he watches the men and young Henry ride away.

CHAPTER 2
Forgotten

The beautiful Champion homestead just ahead is quite the mansion when compared to other homes of the time. The large Spanish style villa with its antique weathered Mediterranean clay roof sits high on a hill overlooking the hill country. Horses and cattle graze in the fields below. Beautiful Texas live oak trees line the entrance road of the ranch.

John Champion has acquired hundreds of thousands of acres that now make up the Champion Ranch. Considering John has no skills in farming, the ranch focuses entirely on cattle production. Besides, John does not have the patience to wait around and watch plants grow.

The sun is beginning to set in the afternoon sky as John Champion and his son Frank ride along the old trail heading back to the Champion ranch. Young Henry rides ahead to the barn to put his horse away for the night.

John Champion's demeanor is silent and stoic. Frank is angry and ready to confront his father.

"I don't want my son involved in your crimes and killings, Father," says Frank. "For that matter, I won't be a part of it either."

"You're a spineless weak man, Frank. I'm embarrassed to say you're my son. Henry will grow up just like you if I don't show him how to be a man," John fires back.

"I hate you, Father," Frank answers quickly. "I won't stand by and watch my son become a murderer and a thief like you!"

"Better than a weak man like you."

"You killed children, Father," Frank yells. "I'm going to the sheriff, or maybe the governor. They will stop you."

Frank begins to ride away from his father as John Champion pulls out his pistol and shoots his son in the back killing him. Frank falls off of his horse and hits the dirt hard. John Champion coldly rides past him without looking back, leaving his son dead and lying face down in the dirt.

Back at the Baker farm, young George gazes about his burned-out homestead, stares blankly with tears still matting his young face.

Nothing remains of his home by the river except for the stone fireplace rising like a monument into the sky. George sits on the hearth and sobs for a while, contemplating what he should do next. George finally stands and lingers about, looking for anything he can save. He does not find much there in the ashes. He remembers an old box that his father had hidden behind one of the stones in the fireplace.   He yanks out the odd stone. The empty space reveals a tarnished metal box which has not been damaged by the fire. As George opens it, he sees some family keepsakes -- his mother's string of pearls, an old pocket watch, and a few pieces of paper that have been safely kept inside. He opens one of the folded papers and reads, '*Land Deed.*' George folds the paper and puts it back in the box. He picks up his rifle, tucks the box under his arm, and wearily walks away from the farm as the blackened remains of his home continue to smolder.

It is almost night-time, and George is exhausted from his long walk. A few miles from home, George heads for a farmhouse in the distance. The light from a gas lantern is seen as George makes his way to his Uncle Wally's small farmhouse. The sounds of the night are beginning to scare young George. A coyote howls nearby and it gets George running.

As George gets closer to his uncle's farm, he begins yelling for him.

"Uncle Wally, Uncle Wally!" George yells as his uncle comes out of his home.

"George! What is it?" Wally responds, as he runs to meet him.

"They killed 'em, Uncle," says George sadly. "They killed 'em all."

"What are you saying, George? What happened?" His uncle is beginning to fear the worst.

Uncle Wally picks up his nephew and carries him into the farmhouse before George can respond. Safely tucked in his Uncle Wally's cot, and with eyes full of tears, George recounts the day's tragic events.

"I'm brokenhearted that you had to witness that horror, George. John Champion will pay for his crimes. We will make him pay. If not in this lifetime, in the next," Uncle Wally says in an angry but devastated tone. Uncle Wally tries to control his tears through the rage he feels for John Champion.

"Get some sleep, George." We will go into town and see the sheriff tomorrow.

"I don't think it will do any good," George mutters back. "Those Champions get away with everything. Henry was there, Uncle. My schoolmate. Henry saw the whole thing."

Forgotten, Texas is a one-horse town in 1928. The remote hill country town is a long day's ride on horseback from the city of San Antonio. The townspeople still use gas lanterns to light their homes at night. They have not seen indoor electric lighting, which was becoming more popular in the United States around this time. Occasionally, a Ford Model T might pass through town. This was somewhat of a treat for the one hundred residents of Forgotten. They could hear the car coming for a mile, and they would come out of their homes and stare in astonishment, and wave at the fortunate driver as he passed through town.

This morning, Uncle Wally and George are riding into Forgotten heading straight to Sheriff Barnum's stone jail house. The jail is the only two-story building in town. The bottom floor serves as an office, and the top floor has one cell for prisoners. As they approach, Sheriff Barnum is sitting on a mesquite bench outside of the jailhouse door. Wally and George dismount and tie their horses to the hitching post.

"Howdy, Baker. Boy. What can I do for ya?" says Sheriff Barnum in a thick Texas drawl, sounding as if he is trying to speak with marbles in his mouth. His thick moustache curls up at the ends like horns.

"You know damn well why we're here!" Uncle Wally says.

"Settle down. Just spit it out, Baker. I ain't in no mood for a guessing game," Sheriff says in a scolding tone.

"Those Champions killed my brother and his family in cold blood. Do somethin' dammit!"

"You got any evidence to what you're saying, Baker?" Sheriff seems impatient.

"George here seen the whole thing."

"Ya did, did ya boy?" Sheriff Barnum stands and says to George with his face lowered down to meet George's gaze.

"Yes, sir. I seen it. Henry was with them, too," George responds standing his ground.

"Baker, ya can't go around defamin' respectable folks like the Champions without some kinda evidence," Sheriff says mockingly.

"Why the hell you protecting 'em, Sheriff? George here saw 'em kill his whole family with his own two eyes."

Uncle Wally's face is sweaty and red as he becomes increasingly frustrated and angry.

"Guess ya better show me the bodies," says the sheriff.

"The... bodies are gone. I want Champion brought in and locked up!"

Sheriff Barnum lazily tosses his hat on the bench and sits back down.

"Like I said, Baker. Ya can't go around like this accusin' folks less ya got ya some evidence. Now if ya find some, ya'll come right back here and see me," Sheriff Barnum says as he gets comfortable on the bench.

Uncle Wally understands that he will not find any justice here. He pushes George out in front of him and they walk away.

"Ain't he gonna do something, Uncle Wally?"

They head back to their horses, mount, and ride away with heavy shoulders. Uncle Wally and George remain silent on the long ride back home to Uncle Wally's farm.

Back in Forgotten, John Champion rides into town. He sits high on his saddle as he stops in front of Sheriff Barnum, now napping on the bench.

"Wake up, Barnum!"

Barnum opens his eyes and smiles. He is really happy to see John Champion it seems.

"Ya got it, John?" Sheriff eagerly asks.

John Champion reaches into a saddlebag and tosses the sheriff a small leather pouch. Sheriff Barnum peeks inside and seems satisfied.

"Things are gettin' out of control around here, John. Ain't ya pillaged enough land by now? Can't protect ya forever," Sheriff says, "Hell, ya got more than ya need!"

"Ain't your business what I got, what I need, or how I get it. And you will do what I say for as long as I tell you, or you and your kin will pay hard," John Champion responds arrogantly.

"Tell ya, John. I might not be around long enough to see it, but you will be the one to pay in hell for all you've done. You have cursed your kin forever."

"You wanna live?" Champion asks Barnum.

John Champion gives him a deadly sneer, turns his horse, and rides away.

Back at Wally Baker's farmhouse, Uncle Wally is lighting a gas lantern by his bed. Young George is sound asleep on a cot nearby. He is shivering and seems to be having a nightmare. Uncle Wally throws an extra blanket on the boy. He sits next to him and looks sadly on his young face for a few moments.

"I can't imagine it, George. Can't imagine the horror of what you've seen," he says quietly to himself.

CHAPTER 3
Daisy

Two boys are rolling around in the dirt fighting as the dust and dirt flies everywhere. One boy tackles the other to the ground, with both boys landing hard on the dirt. There is a small weathered wooden schoolhouse in the background as the boys really go after each other. Hatred emanates from their faces. A few other children surround them, yelling and encouraging the scuffle. George Baker and Henry Champion are the boys engaged in the fight.

"Get 'im, George!" yell the children. "Kick 'im! Henry's just a bully. George, get 'im!"

George scrambles to his feet looking at Henry who he has just knocked down. There is obvious animosity toward Henry on young George's face. George is taking his revenge out on Henry for the recent tragedy they both witnessed. Henry goes for George, but George side steps, knocks him down, and pounces on him. The children continue yelling. The boys are really going at it. Henry pushes George back making George fall into the dirt.

"You stay away from Daisy, or I'll beat you good. You hear me, George?" says Henry gritting his teeth at George.

A pretty, little girl named Daisy stands with the children encouraging George.

"Stop it, Henry!" Daisy yells. "Get up, George. Get up! Get up!"

Daisy's voice slowly comes into sharper focus, and reverbs sounding like a little girl and then changing into the voice of a woman. George is now a grown man sleeping in his bed as his wife comes into the room.

"Wake up, George! Wake up, dear," says Daisy, now a very pretty woman in her mid-30's.

George opens his eyes from his dream to find his wife of thirteen years trying to wake him.

"Wake up, George. Bad dreams again, dear?" she adds.

"Oh. Morning, Daisy," George says trying to gain his bearings.

As Daisy sits on the edge of the bed. George smiles up at her and places a hand on her shoulder and brings her down toward him for a morning kiss.

"Daisy, my love," George continues, as he kisses her sweetly on the lips.

"It's time to get up, George. It's Saturday. You know what that means!"

"Where are the twins?"

"Outside playing somewhere," Daisy says as she stands to leave.

George sits on the edge of the bed and rubs his eyes. A Roy's Feed Store calendar hangs on the wall next to the bed with the year 1950 written on the canvas. Twenty-two years have passed since that horrific morning on his family's farm by the river. George and Daisy now share a nice life together, although the past still haunts George.

"I've got to drive into Forgotten to get some feed from Roy's," says George.

As George stands and looks out of the window, he sees the beautiful countryside. The sun is shining. It is a gorgeous Texas Hill Country day. His twelve-year-old twins, a boy they named Patrick after his father, and a girl named Katie, are happily playing outside riding a horse around. He loves them more than life.

The town of Forgotten has grown up a lot in the past two decades. The feedstore is a busy place this morning. As George exits the store, Roy carries a sack of feed on his shoulder out to George's truck. Roy dumps it on top of several other sacks, and George hops into his 1946 Chevy pickup.

"Thanks for your help, Roy!" George says as he starts his truck.

"No problem, George. See you again soon."

George backs up the truck and heads out of town toward Highway 16. After the rough night and terrible nightmares, he is in a great mood and carefree, whistling to a country tune on the radio as he enjoys the sunny day and beautiful scenery. George is a couple of miles out of town when he sees another truck approaching. It is recognizable, and George suddenly pops a frown on his face. He is no longer whistling.

Approaching in the distance is a brand new, red 1950 Chevy truck. George instantly gets angry, as if someone just turned on a switch, and his good disposition disappears off of his face.

A handsome man also now in his late thirties, Henry Champion, drives toward George. He is sporting a mischievous expression on his face. He wears an expensive Stetson on his head. Henry sees George approaching. He chuckles to himself, and slightly turns the steering wheel. Henry is laughing as he changes lanes, over into George's. Henry is playing 'chicken' with George again. George sees the lane change and the red pickup aimed at him coming closer and closer.

"You've lost your mind, Henry. Not that you ever had one to speak about kindly. You're one sorry son of a b--!" George mutters to himself.

Henry gets closer and closer, and as he does, he becomes happier and happier, his smile growing with every revolution of the tires!   The two trucks are about to collide head-on, as George swerves and drives off the road and into a ditch at the last second. Henry's red pickup zooms on by, and Henry is laughing like crazy and waving like a madman out of his window as he goes past. He is enjoying the fun and sport of it as he drives on down the road.

"You've always been crazy, Henry," George says angrily.

The dust billows around George's truck as he gathers himself and regains his breathing. Although humiliated and shook up, both man and truck are okay. George gears it out of the ditch and continues to the farm.

At the Champion estate, Henry comes up the driveway and gets out. Just moments earlier, Henry had been full of laugher and mischievous play. Now, he is almost stoic and seems incapable of enjoyment. He still lives in his grandfather's estate in which he grew up. The Champion Villa looks none the worse considering a couple of decades have now passed. The trees surrounding the estate are much taller, and the home appears grander than before.

Henry's grandfather, John Champion, had died from a heart attack in his sleep a few years earlier. All of his heinous crimes were buried with him upon his death. Henry always suspected his grandfather had a bad heart from all the drinking, and it had ultimately contributed to his demise.

Inside the estate, Henry now sits alone in a huge and immaculate dining room waiting for lunch. The beautiful cedar and mesquite wood table is capable of sitting ten people, but in all the many years Henry has never had invited guests join him for dinner. His housekeeper, Elena, walks in and out of the room serving him.

"Where's the boy?" Henry asks her.

"Playing outside by the corral," she answers meekly.

"Go find him," Henry orders her sternly.

"Si, senor," says Elena, and obediently heads out of the room.

Henry looks down at his plate of food as if it looks unappetizing, and then stands and leaves the table.

It is a beautiful Sunday along the Rio Frio River. Daisy and George are spreading out a picnic lunch. The twins, Patrick and Katie, are running along the river's edge. An old live oak tree provides some great shade.

"Look kids!" George says calling Patrick and Katie over to him. "This live oak has been on this land for over two hundred and fifty years."

"No kiddin', Dad?" Patrick asks.

"If you look over on the other side, you'll see Jesse James' hancock on it," George adds.

"Jesse James? But the books say he was in Missouri and.... I never heard of him coming to Texas," replies Patrick.

"You're just kidding, huh Dad?" Katie chimes in.

"No, I'm not kidding. You see, that's how little people actually know about the true west. Back then, Texas was the real west, and this is where those outlaws fled to, seeing as it was so close to the Mexican border," George says to his kids.

"Honest?" Patrick asks.

"With a posse coming down on them and all, they had to get away. This was the real West back then," George says emphasizing 'real.'

"The real West," Katie says, imitating him.

Daisy walks up to her family with a cheerful smile.

"What story are you telling the kids now, George?"

"Awww, Daisy. You know I wouldn't lie to the twins."

Daisy gives him the usual warm smile, knowing him too well, as they exchange winks and grins.

Back at the Champion Estate, the house is lit up tonight. Henry and his twelve-year-old son, Daniel, sit at the long dining table having dinner.

"I've told you to stay away from those trashy Baker twins. They're no good," Henry says.

Daniel does not like his father's insults against Patrick and Katie. They are his best friends. He has become used to his father's mood swings.

"They're my friends, Dad."

"Hear me, boy. And I don't want you taking them down to the old stone fireplace by the river. That place is off limits. Do you understand me?!" Henry yells at his son.

Elena is nearby and eyeing them both but keeps working.

"Why are you such a mean bully?" Daniel asks his dad.

"Oh, is that what those trashy Baker kids call me?"

"No... but everyone in town calls you that," Daniel states in a matter of fact tone.

That tweaks Henry a bit, and Elena smiles slightly as she exits into the kitchen.

"Gossip, boy. I'm the boss to most of them and it makes them feel big speaking that way about the ranch owner. I'm just doing what is best for you, Daniel. You have been my responsibility alone ever since your Mama died at Falcon Dam," Henry says to his son.

Henry had originally met Daniel's mother, Olivia, at her husband's funeral. Her husband was a Domador de Caballos, a man who breaks and tames horses for a living. He was killed while being thrown off of a horse and ended up breaking his neck in the process. Olivia was three months pregnant with Daniel at the time. Perhaps out of pity, Henry offered to marry her, and without having any other choices Olivia had agreed to be his wife. He grew fond of her, only to lose her when Daniel was a toddler.

As Henry sits at the table with Daniel now, there is genuine hurt and sadness on his face.

"Just because you don't like George Baker don't mean I can't play with the twins," Daniel says defiantly.

Still thinking about his wife's tragedy, "I should never have taken your Mama out on that boat, knowing she couldn't swim and..." Henry says.

Daniel sees his father's sorrow but finishes his thought.

"If I want to play with Patrick and Katie, that's what I'm gonna do!" Daniel finishes he thought.

"Don't you talk back to me, boy!"

Henry slams his fist on the thick wooden dining table as he furiously stands his chair back and leaves the room. Elena freezes in the doorway to the kitchen as Henry hurries past.

Daniel's eyes are wide, but then he grabs his glass of milk and takes a big swig out of it leaving a milk moustache. He is used to his father's tantrums and smiles at Elena.

The water in the Frio River is nice and cool today. Although having been previously warned, days later the kids are at the river again. Daniel, Katie, and Patrick are having a great time swimming. The old stone fireplace looms nearby. The children are unaware of the tragedy that occurred at this very location all those many years ago. Daniel is singing a tune, and Katie and Patrick join in. It is obvious young Daniel has a talent for singing. It is also apparent these kids are great friends.

"I'm going to get us some oranges from your Dad's grove, Champ," Patrick announces to Daniel.

"Be careful, Patrick, he's got eyes everywhere."

"I'll be quiet as a cat in a field of mice," Patrick says, as he runs from the river and disappears through the brush and trees.

"My top!" Katie suddenly shrieks as she turns away from Daniel.

Katie ducks in lower into the river, turning around looking for her top.

"I'll help you find it, Katie," Daniel says, trying to help.

"Daniel, please! Turn around!"

Daniel freezes, holds up his hands, nods and turns around.

"Okay, okay," Daniel grins.

Katie looks over and sees it, snatches it up and puts it back on under the water.

As Daniel turns back to face her, his look is different, and he feels something about Katie and himself he has never experienced before. Katie notices his expression. For a quick moment they share a look and discover one another. But the moment is broken when Patrick runs toward the river. He carries several oranges in his hands. He trips and stumbles into the water and the oranges go flying from his hands.

"Okay folks, whattam I bid for these lovely oranges from the grove of Henry Champion?

Do I hear five—I wanna five, five, five. Do I hear six? Six, six, six," Patrick says while laughing.

CHAPTER 4
1956

Six years have now passed, and the Forgotten Auction is a busy place, as it is every day. The little town of Forgotten has grown some, and ranchers from miles away habitually find themselves at the auction buying and selling their stock. The auctioneer is rattling away in a language of his own, as ranchers and farmers are filling up the stands, listening, watching, and waiting for their picks to come up.

George Baker is sitting with some of the men, checking his list and observing carefully. Henry Champion is also in attendance and sitting across the aisle from George. It appears Henry is as interested in George and his bids, as he is in the livestock up for auction. Everyone around them can sense the palpable hatred between them. Each time George raises his hand in a bid, Henry outbids him. They exchange eye contact frequently during the bidding, and there is glee in Henry's eyes as he outbids George every time. When the bidding is done, Henry tips his expensive black Stetson at George, and sends him the usual smirk George has come to know.

At the end of the auction day, George ends up with the least desirable cattle. Defeat is written all over his face. On the other hand, Henry is triumphant. George is obviously seething inside but cannot do much about Henry's money and his ability to purchase the best livestock on the auction block.

It is a magnificent day at Forgotten High School. The newly built white stone building on the school's campus is the largest structure in town. With a train now stopping close to town for cattle loading, the town has become a hub for the cattle industry in the region, and many new families have moved into Forgotten in the past couple of years. This growth in population required a new high school as the town had outgrown the old one.

Katie, Patrick and Daniel, now high school seniors, are distracted and not paying attention to Mrs. Rogers. The Math teacher has a scowl on her face as she confronts the trio.

"Would you please answer the question, Daniel?"

Daniel has been staring at Katie and gulps as he realizes he is in trouble. He has not been paying attention at all and has no idea what is going on in class. Patrick, sitting behind Daniel, laughs at his best friend. Daniel has grown up to be a handsome young man. He has had eyes for the lovely Katie and no one else since he was twelve.

Katie, seeing Daniel's predicament, decides to save him. "I know the answer, Mrs. Rogers," she says to her teacher.

Mrs. Rogers is not going to let Daniel off the hook that easily. She sees Patrick snickering and grinning and turns her attention to him next.

"Well then maybe Patrick knows the answer," the teacher quips quickly.

The entire class is laughing at them now. Mrs. Rogers throws an eraser at Patrick's head, who is now laughing his head off. In an unlikely good turn, Mrs. Rogers seems to be in a decent mood today and laughs along with her class. Rarely, the erasers miss their target, but not today. If anyone dared to get caught sleeping in her class, an eraser thrown their way from across the room would surely wake them up.

Katie looks out of the classroom window and notices her dad driving by in his truck towing a trailer headed home from the auction.

The Baker farmhouse has some added growth these six years later. There are more wild daisies and impatiens in the yard. The house and barn have recently been painted a rusty brown color. Majestic green Texas live oaks, mesquite trees, cedar trees, and shrubbery extend far into the countryside surrounding the farm. Uncle Walley's tiny old, weathered farmhouse can be seen in the near distance not far from the main farmhouse. George thinks on his Uncle Wally now and does not know where he would have gone if he had not had his uncle. He was a good man and raised George to be kind and hard-working. His dying many years back hit George extremely hard. Uncle Wally and George were men carved from the same piece of stone. He missed his uncle greatly.

George drives up to the farm and pulls close to the barn with the trailer. Daisy comes out of the house and walks over to greet him with a glass of lemonade.

"How did it go, dear? Did you get the ones you wanted?" she asks with hesitation in her voice.

"No, Daisy. I don't think that's going to happen in this lifetime. I should stick to farming," George responds in a matter-of-fact tone.

George lets out a scraggly cow, pats it on the butt, and sends it on its way into the corral. He and Daisy head to the front porch.

"Let me guess, Henry?" she asks as they sit down.

"Yea.... The most money generally wins the game. And buying cattle's just a game," George says.

"I don't understand why no one stands up to that bully. He goes around like he's king of the hill," Daisy says frustrated.

"Daisy, I've told you before. If we stay out of his way, he will leave us alone."

"Whatever you say, George," Daisy says giving up. She knows George well, and it is a touchy subject.

"The older Champion gets, the crazier he becomes. I don't want my family hurt."

Daisy remains silent for a moment. She understands the pain that George has been through in his life, the pain that comes from losing family. In George's case, his entire family but for his Uncle Wally.

"Well, it seems to me he hurts one member of this family nearly every day," she says.

"Besides being the prettiest woman I've ever known, you're also the most relentless. Just stay out of his way, honey. That is all there is to do." Daisy's stare is making George feel uncomfortable and his cheeks twitch when he smiles.

"Mighty good lemonade, my love," George says while raising his glass and offering a grin and a toast to Daisy as he stands and goes in the door.

"Sure, he'll leave you alone. That will be the day, George Baker," Daisy mutters to herself.

A shiny new Champion Ranch pickup truck complete with the ranch logo drives along the opposite side of some fencing along George's farm. Some of the fence is in bad need of repair. The truck passes on by and then puts on its brakes and stops. The truck backs up to the weak fencing and Henry's men see some cattle grazing within. Two of Henry's men get out of the truck and check out the fence.

"Look here... the fence on Baker's land is about to come down," Willy Watson says while snickering.

Johnny Spader and Willy Watson laugh out loud. "Yeah... Baker's *pinche* few head of cattle could end up over her on Champion land," Johnny Spader says while pulling at the fencing and bringing it down.

"What a shame," Willy says. "Baker needs to get busy fixing his fence or he's going to lose his cattle," he adds while laughing, as a section of the old fence completely falls.

They proceed to shove and push George's cattle over into Henry's land, all the while enjoying themselves tremendously. They laugh at their evil doings, get in the truck, and drive away.

CHAPTER 5
Young Love

It is an early Friday night as George's Chevy pickup pulls into the pump island at Lozano's Grocery Store and Gas. The twins, Patrick and Katie, are in the cab with Patrick driving. Coming in from the other direction is a brand new, 1956 Chevy pickup. Daniel Champion roars his truck into the pump on the opposite side of Patrick. The gas attendant, Joe, runs over to Patrick's driver side window.

"Filler up?" Joe says to Patrick.

"Yeah, Joe. Thanks," he says. "I'm going over to talk to Champ," Patrick says to Katie as he gets out of the truck.

Katie is sitting in the truck eyeing Daniel, who is returning her look. Patrick leans on Daniel's window. He observes Daniel and his sister checking each other out.

"Pretty fine," Patrick says to Daniel admiring his truck.

"She sure is," Daniel says with his eyes on Katie.

"Talking about your truck, Champ."

"Yea, early graduation present from the old man."

Katie sits looking pretty in the cab, becoming shy and embarrassed by Daniel's attention.

"It ain't no secret you're fond of my sister, Champ. Why don't you ask her to go riding around tonight? I've got a feeling she'd say yes."

"You think?" Daniel asks.

"Friday night... and there's a full moon," Patrick says egging on his best friend. Daniel is unsure, looking at Katie.

"Tempting, but you know how the folks feel about us all hanging out. My father's crap would hit the fan if he found out I was dating your sister."

"Since when have we given a frog's butt what your father thinks? Just go over and ask her out."

Daniel nervously gets out and walks to the old truck and finds himself in front of Katie's window. She smiles at him.

"Wow, she's so beautiful," Daniel thinks to himself.

"Hey, Champ!"

"Hi, Katie. I was just thinking... uhhh."

"It's about time!" Katie sweetly says to
him, bringing a big smile to Daniel's face.

It is only nine in the morning and already
beginning to get warm as George rides along his
property line on his horse. He is enjoying this
beautiful morning. He is proud of the work he
has done to build up his farm. About fifteen
hundred acres are entirely for crops, and five
hundred acres are for the small herd of fifty
head of cattle and a handful of horses he owns.

As George rides, he notices the cattle tracks
going from his land, through the broken fence,
and onto Henry's ranch. He can also make out
boot prints and tire tracks on the other side of
the fence. George looks with disgust in the
direction of the Champion estate. He is fuming
and stomps back to his horse.

"I've just about had enough of you, Henry!"
George mutters to himself. "You're gonna pay."

George pulls on the horse's reins and rides off.

Sheriff Pete is a big, tall Texan, at least 6 and a half feet tall. At the present, he is the only one there of his four-man office, going over some files at a cabinet. He is a good-hearted soul and is much loved and respected by the citizens of Forgotten. The door to the office opens and George walks in. George is still as angry as he was earlier.

"Howdy there, George. What brings you into my office today?" Sheriff Pete says to George.

Hot and sweaty, George answers him with two words. "One guess."

"Not again," Sheriff Pete mutters under his breath.

"Some of my cattle is missing. Five, maybe as many as ten. It has Champion's fingerprints all over it. I would like you to come out to Henry's estate with me," George says firmly to Pete.

Pete sighs, and without hesitation, he grabs his cowboy hat, and they head out.

"We'll take my patrol car," Pete says to George.

They drive out of town headed toward the Champion estate. It is a quiet ride, neither wanting to say much.

The estate stands high on a rise in the distance. Elena, Henry's housekeeper, is busy with chores as George and Pete pull up into the driveway. Elena still works for the Champions, having remained in Henry's good graces all these years. George and Sheriff Pete get out of the patrol car and head for the eight-foot-tall ornately carved front doors. Henry had purchased the doors in Mexico, complete with the heavy brass door knocker.

"Let me handle this, George. You know you get feisty and it gets us nowhere."

"Hot, ain't it?" Sheriff Pete adds, with a nervous tone in his voice as he knocks on one of the doors.

You can tell Pete is not happy to be there. Confronting Henry is the last thing he feels like doing today, or on any other day.

Elena answers the door to greet them.

"Buenos dias, Elena. Esta el Señor?" Pete asks her.

Elena responds softly and with much elegance, "Un momento, por favor."

They remain outside at the door as Elena runs to fetch Henry. After a few minutes, Henry appears before them.

"What can I do for you, Sheriff," Henry says, obviously ignoring George.

"George here says you may have some of his cattle," Pete replies hesitantly.

"Is this a polite way of asking if I stole George's cows again, Sheriff?"

Sheriff merely shrugs off the query, and before he can speak again, Henry says, "I got a receipt for those horns, Pete. Be happy to show you. C'mon inside. You, too, George," he adds, giving George the usual nasty smirk.

George and Pete exchange a look as they come into a grand entry. They follow Henry down a long hallway and into Henry's library which serves as his office. It is a magnificent room. Rich wood panels adorn the walls and ceilings, leather everywhere, and a painting of Henry's grandfather, John Champion, is mounted above the large mantle of a grand river rock and stone fireplace. John's harsh and malevolent expression in the painting is anything but inviting in this cold, expansive room. Henry goes around his desk where he pulls out a file and produces some documents for Sheriff Pete.

"You see, Sheriff. I can account for everything," Henry says as he hands over the documents. "Bill of sale on my cattle and you'll find it a legitimate business transaction," Henry adds smugly.

"Pete, there is no Bill of Sale 'cause I didn't sell him a damn thing," George cries out angrily.

"Well, this seems to be okay," Sheriff Pete says to Henry.

The sheriff hands the paperwork back to Henry as George sends a hateful, dirty look toward Henry, and storms out of the room.

"When is it going to end, Henry?" Pete says.

Sheriff Pete shakes his head and follows George out of the house. George is already sitting in the patrol car as Pete gets in.

"How the heck can you let him get away with this," George says angrily.

"If I had real evidence against him, I wouldn't," Pete answers.

"Evidence. Another Sheriff said the same thing to my Uncle Wally and me when I was a kid," George replies.

"George, you have to be patient. Henry is going to get what's coming to him. Sooner or later, he is going to pay," Sheriff says calmly.

They drive away from the Champion estate as Henry stands by his window and laughs his head off at George, catching George's eye. As they pull away from the house, George seethes inside watching Henry's display of pure evil. He has witnessed this same behavior from Henry all of his life.

"It's only a matter of time, George. His high and mighty throne is going to buck him off."

As expected, Sheriff Pete's words provide no comfort for George. They drive back to town in silence. Sheriff Pete feels badly for George. It is hard to witness a good man like George being constantly ridiculed and humiliated by Henry.

CHAPTER 6
It Begins

A full moon is big and bright in the night sky and its shadow dances on the water. It is a beautiful night at the river, and the moon really lights up the landscape. Daniel and Katie are leaning against his truck by the water. His arms are around Katie's waist.

"Are you my girl?" Daniel asks Katie sweetly.

"I'm your girl," Katie replies. "Are you my guy?"

"I'm your man!" Daniel says happily. "Will you come with me to San Antonio tomorrow night to see Jack Nelson in concert?"

"Yes," Katie says without hesitation.

Katie and Daniel are silhouetted against the moon. He takes her face in his hands and kisses her. Their world is genuinely perfect right now. It seems nothing could ever change the feelings they have for each other. It is late at night when Daniel heads back to the Champion Ranch. A country song plays on the radio. Daniel sings along to the tune. He is smiling and happy as he heads down the driveway into the estate.

As he gets closer to the house, he notices Henry sitting on the front steps holding a bottle of whiskey in his hand. Daniel knows this could be either a good or bad encounter with his father. He just never knows which way it is going to go, but usually it is rotten.

"Hello, Father."

"Nice night, huh, Danny?"

"Yea, fine night. What are you still doing up?" Daniel asks, not really sure he wants to hear the answer.

"A weakness of mine, worrying about you. Can a man wait up for his only son?"

Daniel sees the whiskey bottle in his father's hand and realizes Henry is intoxicated again.

There is resentment in his voice as Daniel says, "I'm not your son."

Daniel has spent his entire life embarrassed to have any relationship to a drunk. For as long as he can remember, Henry has made it a habit of showing up intoxicated to Daniel's school sporting events. Daniel would watch in shame each time Henry would attend, listening to his father drunkenly shouting from the bleachers.

One football Friday night a few years back, a drunken Henry actually fell coming down the bleachers and hurt his knee and back. It was one of Daniel's most embarrassing moments, as the crowd watched him run off the football field to see if his father was okay. They had to stop the game clock while Henry was tended to by a doctor and then taken away.

Clearly hurt by Daniel's comment, "You're my son in every way that matters when I adopted you as a baby."

Losing patience with his father, "Quit sucking on that bottle and go to bed. C'mon, I'll help you, Dad."

As Daniel reaches to help him up, he notices blood on his father's pants.

"You've been out deer hunting again, haven't you, Dad?"

Henry ignores the question, takes another swig from his bottle.

"Season's over, Father. You know it's not legal."

"Full moon," Henry replies.

"It doesn't matter," Daniel says, clearly done with him.

"I'll never let you bring that nasty Baker girl around here," Henry says coldly. "And that brother of hers is no better. They're both losers and trash. All of those Bakers are worthless."

Daniel pauses as if to say something, decides it is not worth the effort and heads up the steps to go inside.

"You hear me, boy!" Henry yells, as he remains sitting on the steps and continues to drink out of his bottle.

Daniel and Katie are enjoying the hill country drive this beautiful spring day as they head to San Antonio for Jack Nelson's concert tonight. The highway is flanked by gorgeous bluebonnets on both sides of the road, and the fields are also drenched in blue as flowers fill the horizon as far as the eye can see. Katie sits closely to Daniel in the truck, his hand wrapped around hers.

"Stop staring at me, Champ! Keep your eyes on the road, or there will be no concert tonight!"

Daniel obeys and focuses on his driving for a short while. Soon enough though, he finds himself glancing at Katie once again.

A new music artist is just now hitting the music scene in 1956. Elvis Presley's hit song, '*I Forgot to Remember*,' plays on the radio and Daniel and Katie happily sing along. They eye each other often, with their hearts full of young love for one another.

It is now Saturday night and the concert hall in San Antonio is packed with people enjoying Jack Nelson up on stage. Daniel and Katie are cheering right along with the crowd having the time of their lives. They both feel like life cannot get any better for them. Jack Nelson plays the last song of the night with his band.

"Do you think I could be this good, Katie?" Daniel asks her.

"If that's what you really want. Yea, of course you can," Katie says confidently.

As the last song is coming to an end, Daniel stands and says to Katie, "I want to meet Jack, come with me."

Daniel takes Katie by the hand and walks through the crowd as they make their way toward the back of the concert hall. A security guard suddenly stops them, and proceeds to push them away. At that precise moment, Jack Nelson walks down the stairs with other security in tow.

"What's going on?" Jack Nelson asks the guard.

"These kids were trying to get back here. I'll get them out of here," the guard says nervously, as if he has been caught not doing his job.

"Just wanted to meet you, Mr. Nelson. I'm a big fan... and I'm a country singer, too," Daniel says to Jack Nelson.

"Is that right," Jack Nelson says with a big grin.

"He really is," Katie chimes in.

"Yea, I have a band, and I sing and play guitar. Although, I'll never be as good as you, Mr. Nelson."

"I don't know about that. What's your name?"

"Daniel Champion, Sir. And this is my girlfriend, Katie Baker."

Jack Nelson offers Daniel and Katie a warm handshake.

"Well, Daniel. First of all. You can just call me Jack. And second of all, if you want it, you work hard and go for it."

"Yes, sir... Jack."

"But you know, this life isn't all it's cracked up to be. You have to keep a level head. And you always have to remember the word 'honor.' It is the easiest word to forget in this business."

Daniel is extremely focused on Jack. Katie has never seen this side of Daniel.

Jack continues, "And the best piece of advice I can give you... never choose fame over love. Never. Nice meeting you both."

Jack Nelson and his entourage walk away leaving Daniel and Katie staring back at them. Suddenly Jack Nelson turns around and yells at them.

"Hey, Daniel. Want to come on my tour bus and play a couple of songs with me?"

Without answering him, Daniel and Katie look at each other, smile, and run to catch up to the group.

Jack and his entourage enter the tour bus with Daniel and Katie in tow. Only an extraordinarily successful country star could afford this spectacular 1956 Vistaliner Motorcoach in which they now find themselves. Daniel and Katie look around in awe. As the kids get comfortable, someone hands Daniel a guitar. Daniel is clearly on cloud nine. Katie looks at him proudly as she sits next to him and thinks to herself how at home Daniel seems here. Daniel belongs in this world. This realization makes her nervous, as she assumes she will probably lose Daniel one day to his music and to this life. Jack Nelson and Daniel sing a couple of songs together. It is clear Daniel has a lot of talent, and everyone there can see it, too.

As they are getting up to leave Daniel says, "Thanks so much for letting us join you."

"It was fun having you guys. You're really talented, Daniel. Take care, and good luck to you," Jack says giving the kids a hug goodbye.

"I had a great time. Really appreciated this."

"Remember what I said, Daniel. You don't want this unless you're prepared to give up something even bigger for it," Jack says in a more serious tone.

Daniel nods his head, and he and Katie head out of the coach. They stand on the sidewalk and watch as the grand tour bus pulls away.

"What just happened?" Daniel screams happily.

The kids run down the sidewalk holding hands while screaming and laughing!

Being a small town, Forgotten does not have a store for tuxedo nor gowns for kids to wear for prom night. The well-to-do families in town drive into San Antonio and find their tuxedos and elegant gowns in the fancy boutiques and stores. But for most of the kids at Forgotten High School, the local seamstress sews many of the dresses the girls will wear, and she places orders for tuxedos from a store in San Antonio after carefully taking the boy's measurements.

The next day, Patrick and Katie are driving through town on their way to get fitted for Patrick's tux and Katie's gown. As they approach the shop and get out, Henry drives past them in his suburban. When Patrick and Katie catch his eyes, he gives them a loathsome stare that cuts right through them. A chill runs down Katie's back.

"Same ole' Henry," Patrick says to his sister.

"Can't believe Dad has had to put up with him all these years. What a jerk!" Katie replies.

Katie's heart sinks as she thinks about Daniel, and what he must endure on a daily basis having to live with that nut job.

"Biggest jerk around these parts," Patrick agrees.

"Poor Daniel."

Henry's truck speeds away from them as they head inside the shop.

High School Senior Prom Night is here! The Baker farmhouse is all lit up as Katie and Patrick are about to head out for the evening.

George and Daisy are teasing Patrick about how great he looks in his tuxedo.

"Who are you? Do I know you?" George teases his son.

"Not bad for a farm boy, huh?" Patrick says priming.

They look over to see Katie as she comes into the room. Katie sees her handsome brother all dressed up like she has never seen him before.

"Wow, look at you, brother!"

Patrick playfully struts his stuff for the ladies as George smiles at Katie.

"Wow! Look at my beautiful little girl! You look so grown up!"

"Thank you, Dad!"

George adds, "Please tell me you won't be out with that Champion boy?"

"I'm meeting Daniel there. Yes, Papa," Katie answers honestly.

"I've told you to stay away from him, honey," George says to Katie.

"I'm 18 and I can do as I please," Katie says firmly but with love in her voice. "It's not our fault that you and Henry hate each other, Dad."

George is sulking but does not respond. He knows that forbidding her Daniel's company will only alienate her from them. He is praying this childhood crush will end once Katie leaves for college. He also worries about Henry hurting his children.

"I want you kids home by midnight, you hear me?"

"Oh, George c'mon now. It's prom night. They will be home soon enough. Have a good time, kids. Please be safe," Daisy says.

George and Daisy follow them outside and look at them with melancholy looks on their faces. They both wonder where the time has gone, the kids have grown up so fast.

As Patrick and Katie drive away, Patrick yells back at his parents through the open truck window, "See you, two! Love you!"

Katie's waving wildly and blowing kisses at her parents. George and Daisy cannot help but feel immensely proud of the twins as they head back inside.

"Such fine children," Daisy says.

"That's 'cause of the fine job you've done raising them, Daisy," George says kissing her lips.

"I did have some help. You're a heck of a man, George Baker," Katie says putting her arms around his neck.

"That's exactly what you said to me when I asked you to marry me all those years ago. Have you enjoyed your life with me, Daisy?"

"It's been grand, George. I love you."

"Have I ever told you what an incredible woman you are, Daisy Baker?"

"Oh, I think you've mentioned it a time or two these past 19 years," Daisy says gushing like a teenager.

After all these years of marriage, George can still make her feel like a schoolgirl in love.

"You're a stunning woman. Henry has never had squat to be jealous of me about... except for one thing – you!" George says flirting with her.

"Oh, George!"

George heads over to an old victrola and changes the record. He chooses their favorite song by Pat Suzuki, *'How High the Moon.'* The singer's haunting voice fills the room. Each word she sings holds a special meaning for them both. The sun has now set, and twilight fills the room. The hazy lighting and dreamy music has George in a romantic mood.

"May I have this dance, Mrs. Baker?" George asks, bowing like a gentleman to Daisy.

They smile at each other, kiss, and then snuggle closely as they sway to the music. The scratchy song plays as they look out into the night through the window with the curtains blowing slightly in the hill country breeze.

CHAPTER 7
An Unforgettable Night

Forgotten High School is an exciting place tonight as seniors arrive for their high school prom. A country song plays loudly as the doors to the rotunda open and close each time new kids arrive and make their way inside. Daniel is dressed handsomely in a black tux and black Stetson hat. He picks at his guitar and begins singing a popular country song. He is joined by his band, made up of some of his life-long friends. Daniel is singing now as Katie and Patrick make their entrance. Patrick find his date, Beth, and quickly pulls her out on the dance floor. Daniel sends a happy look Katie's way. Daniel is so blown away by the way Katie looks, he stumbles and forgets the lyrics to the song.   After a few minutes, the song ends. Daniel makes his way to Katie as the band continues playing without him.

"You look so beautiful, Katie," Daniel says admiring her, as he pulls her into his arms for a dance.

"So do you, Champ. Nice tux. You sure clean up nicely for a country boy."

Some of their classmates, Andy Cruz and his date, Becky, also dance along beside them.

"The guys and I are going to go swimming at the river tonight. I'd like to see you. Do you want to take a late-night drive with me later?" Daniels asks.

Katie is quick to say yes. They dance closely cheek to cheek. Katie has never been happier in her life than she is now. The song ends and it is time for Daniel to get back on stage. He gives Katie a quick kiss and then joins his buddies on stage. She really loves watching him perform. Daniel seems to light up in front of a crowd and the look on his face says he loves making people happy with his band's music.

The prom is a success, and it is now time for everyone to get out of there. As kids are piling out of the rotunda, Patrick yells out to Andy.

"You comin' with us, Andy?" Patrick asks?

"Yea, sure!" Andy replies.

Becky elbows Andy hard in the ribs and gives him a hard look of there is no way you will be going anywhere with them.

"Guess not, Patrick!" Andy adds.

After a few laughs and cackling chicken sounds

from the guys Andy says, "Great singing tonight, Daniel!"

They all unanimously say, "Yea, Daniel, great job!"

"We can all say we knew you when!" Andy adds.

"Well, we're gonna go. See you at the graduation picnic on Sunday!" Andy says as he and Becky walk away.

"Helluva, night! Your beast gassed up, Champ?" Patrick yells.

"All set!"

Both Katie and Beth yell out, "We want to come, too!"

They continue toward Daniel's truck, and Patrick removes the keys to the old Chevy from his pocket and tosses them to Katie.

"This is our last night to be boys, Katie. After tonight, we're men!" Patrick jumps into Daniel's truck.

"Sorry, Katie." Daniel kisses her. "Only men allowed."

"Okay, Beth and I will go over to Mary Lou's graduation party and meet up with you later."

"We'll catch up with you both at the tracks around midnight," Daniel says to Katie giving her a kiss goodbye.

Some of the other boys are jumping into the back of Daniel's truck, whoopin' and hollerin' while removing their black ties and jackets.

"We'll see you girls later," Patrick says.

Daniel gives Katie one more kiss, as does Patrick with Beth.

One of the guys in the back yells, "Enough of that shit, Champ! Vamonos!"

"See you at midnight," Katie yells out to Daniel. "Please be careful!"

"You're all nuts!" Beth yells to them.

Daniel roars his beast to life, backs out, and screeches away. The guys in the back of the truck are already cracking beers and yelling.

"Our men are real mature, huh?" Beth says.

"Mature men! Ha! Now there's an oxymoron!"

The girls laugh as they jump in the old Chevy and drive away.

The Champion estate is lit up this late evening as Henry and his men, Johnny Spader and Willy Watson, join him in the library.

"I'm sick of looking at his face!" Henry says to them.

"Maybe you can buy him out," Willy says.

"Maybe the right money would make him sell real fast," Johnny adds.

"George Baker's never had a pot to piss in. You'd think he would sell," Henry replies to them. "Na... he's mighty righteous. He doesn't care about money. Got his little piece of dirt and got Daisy."

As Henry turns to look at his grandfather's painting, "Course, we know there are ways."

Henry pours himself another shot and offers the same to Willy and Johnny.

"When Baker croaks, you could buy the land from the woman," Johnny says to Henry.

"Hell, yeah. What's that pendeja gonna do with it anyway?" Willy adds.

"Willy-muchacho!" With eyes bulging, Henry barks at Willy.

Henry startles the heck out of Willy and adds, "You ever talk like that about Daisy Baker, I'll hurt you good. You hear?"

The water in the Frio River is nice and warm. Daniel, Patrick, and the boys are swimming and drinking their beer. They laugh and holler as they are having the time of their lives. They throw beer cans around to each other, popping them in each other's faces and watching them explode. It is beginning to get late. Gradually, one by one, they begin to get out of the river. The boys put their clothes on over their wet underwear with not a care in the world. Considering the boys rarely drink, Patrick and Daniel are intoxicated. They make their way to the truck and pile in. Daniel speeds off down the road. A country song blares loudly on the radio as the boys sing along. It is a popular song, perfect for driving down the road, and now every boy is singing along.

"We're going to feel like crap in the morning, Champ!" Patrick says to Daniel. "I'm going to get in so much trouble if I get home looking like this!"

"Speak for yourself! I ain't even buzzed," Daniel replies.

They are both laughing and not paying attention to the road. They slap hands, but when they do, Daniel swerves and misses the sharp curve in the road just ahead. The truck spins out of control. Suddenly, Daniel's new pickup dips into the roadside ditch, turns over and goes flying. Boys' bodies fly out of the back. The truck hits the ground and rolls. After a few moments, it is very quiet. The only sound you hear is the hooting of two owls having a conversation. The stillness is soon broken by the noises of boys crying and moaning in pain.

Katie and Beth are waiting patiently by the railroad tracks, expecting Daniel and Patrick to arrive.

"It's after one, Beth. I'm scared."

"What on earth are they doing? Did they forget about us? We're going to get into so much trouble," Beth responds.

Back at the Champion estate, Henry is having one of his usual nightmares. It is the same recurring dream. In his nightmare, Henry is screaming for help as he holds the dead body of his beloved wife, Olivia, as he carries her out of the lake in his arms. He continues to scream for help, only to awaken violently. Henry looks distraught, as he sits up in his bed shaking with fear. His face is damp with tears and sweat.

Henry is now wide awake and having horrible memories. He thinks of his grandmother, Mary, John Champion's wife. He loved her, and he recalls she suddenly disappeared one day when he was about eight years old. He remembers going around the entire estate and barns looking for her, and remembers his grandfather saying she had run away. He clearly remembers asking his grandfather if he was going to go look for her, and John Champion saying his grandmother did not want to be found.

Throughout his life, Henry wondered if his grandfather had killed her, after all, it was not beneath him to do so. He had personal testimony of his grandfather's crimes.
Henry also now thinks of his mother, Ruth,

Frank's wife, who had died in childbirth when Henry was born. It was sad he never knew his mother. Strange, he thought, all the women in his family had been lost to him.

Katie and Beth still wait by the railroad tracks for Daniel and Patrick to return. Finally! Headlights are headed their way. The headlamps shine brightly as they approach.

"It's getting so late. My dad is going to freak," Katie says to Beth.

As the lights get closer, the girls notice it is Sheriff Pete's patrol car pulling up alongside them.

"Oh, crap. It's Sheriff Pete," Beth mutters.

The girls sit innocently in the cab as Pete walks up to the truck. A train whistle is heard approaching in the distance as Pete comes around to Katie's window.

"Hi, Sheriff Pete," the girls say almost in unison.

"Girls."

Sheriff Pete has a long look on his face. He looks sad and apprehensive.

"Katie... Beth... You girls need to get home."

Katie can sense something is terribly wrong.

"What's wrong? Where's Patrick? Is he alright?"

"The boys were drinking, Katie," Pete begins.

"What happened, Sheriff?" Beth asks.

"I'm so sorry, Katie. Beth. Patrick's been killed. Daniel was driving, but he is okay. Katie, I need you to get home. I'll come with you."

Sheriff Pete's face reflects profound sadness. Katie and Beth are both sobbing hysterically at this point. Katie opens her mouth to scream, but nothing comes out. Beth is crying.

"The other boys are okay, just bruised up badly," Pete adds.

The train is getting closer. We hear it thunder on by as Katie's mouth opens to scream, but nothing comes out. She is visibly in shock.

Except for the sound of the chirping birds, Forgotten Cemetery is very peaceful and quiet this day. A breeze blows from the east, and the tall sunflowers in the brush gracefully sway in the wind. Several townspeople are walking away from a freshly dug gravesite. There are many other tombstones in the Forgotten Cemetery, commemorating a long history of the town's past inhabitants. Standing somberly by Patrick's gravesite are George, Daisy, and Katie. The casket has not been lowered and sits on display. The local citizens stop by to pay their respects. George is trying to be strong for his family, although he appears to be more shook up than Daisy, who is inconsolable. Katie appears dazed and in shock. The peaceful sound of the wind and birds chirping is broken by a man's harsh voice.

"My sincerest sympathies to your family, George," Henry says, trying to sound kind.

George's eyes dart toward Henry. Henry is dressed in a dark suit, and appears very discomforted and awkward, as he removes his hat.

"I'm terribly sorry for your pain, Daisy. Katie," Henry adds, looking at them.

"Best you go now, Henry," George says to him.

"If there's anything I can do to help... with the burying expenses or—" Henry politely asks.

"We don't need your charity, Champion. You're not welcomed here!" George is angry and in pain. "Your kin has once again taken from my family."

Henry looks at Daisy and a different look is exchanged between them.

"I'm very sorry for your loss, Daisy," Henry says as he goes to leave.

Daisy says nothing and offers no expression to share with Henry.

"I said go, Champion," George is getting fed up with Henry. It does not take much to trigger George when Henry is around. George feels it is a great disrespect for him to show his face here now.

Just then George's eyes shift to see Daniel walking up. He stops near Henry. His arm is in a sling, with cuts and bruises all over his face and head. Daniel's eyes are moist, and he can barely speak. He is sobbing as he walks over to Katie.

"Katie," Daniel says, standing before her now.

Katie looks at Daniel with the same hard eyes as her dad.

"What are you doing here?! How dare you! You have no right!" Katie yells at Daniel.

"Please Katie, I want to explain."

"You killed Patrick! There's nothing you can say to change that!"

Daniel is having a hard time holding back the tears. He has not stopped crying for several days and his eyes are huge and swollen.

"Let's go son," Henry says to Daniel.

"Don't ever come back, Daniel. I never want to see you again." George shouts out after him.

"Katie, it was an accident. I'm so sorry!" Daniel says yelling her way.

"Get him out of here, Henry!" George says sternly.

Henry puts his arm around Daniel and walks away. Father and son head down the hill on the caliche road. The Forgotten Cemetery is now a short distance behind them. With tears still in his eyes, Daniel looks back over his shoulder at Katie. He notices she is sobbing in her mother's arms. It seems things will never be the same again.

CHAPTER 8
August 1976

Twenty years have passed, and Katie Baker has grown up to be a gorgeous woman. The Los Angeles Courthouse is a busy place as Katie runs up the steps, long brown hair flying, obviously late to court. She is dressed in a blue business suit and heels and carries a briefcase in one hand. In the other, she holds some papers as she walks into the courtroom out of breath. Judge Earl has a snarl on his face and gives Katie a gesture of disapproval.

"Katie Baker, on behalf of the defendant, Your Honor. Sorry I'm late." Katie says with some authority. "The defendant moves for a continuance. The case has just been assigned and we need more time to adequately prepare."

"Is there a written motion, Counselor?" Judge Earl asks.

Thomas Carnegie, the opposing attorney, smirks at Katie. Katie hands the Judge and the opposing attorney a copy of the written motion.

"Mr. Carnegie?" Judge Earl asks.

"This motion was filed stamped three minutes ago, Your Honor. This is not proper notice."

"It's within a court's discretion to grant or deny a continuance at any time," Katie snaps back at Carnegie.

"That is true, Ms. Baker, however, given the..." Carnegie begins...

"Your Honor. Are you going to allow opposing counsel to dictate to this court which rules apply?" Katie argues.

The Judge looks at both lawyers, then says, "Be a little more judicious next time, Ms. Baker."

Thomas Carnegie shoots Katie a victory smile before Judge Earl adds, "Continuance granted."

"But your honor—" Carnegie says defeated.

"I've ruled, Mr. Carnegie," Judge states with a final tone.

"Thank you, Your Honor," Katie says gratefully.

Thomas Carnegie and Katie walk out of the courtroom and stop.

"Well, you won this round, Katie," Thomas says.

"This round? What do you mean this round?"

"Yea, okay. I've been off my game lately."

"You are so much fun to play with, Tommy," Katie says teasing him.

They exchange a look of friendship. Although they find themselves in opposite corners at times, they are close friends.

"It's tough going up against a good friend, isn't it?" Thomas says.

"Na," Katie answers. "It's just tough losing to one. See ya! Love ya!"

Thomas laughs and shakes his head as she blows him a friendly kiss and they go their separate ways.

The L.A. County Music Hall is hopping tonight, and a lot of people are dressed in their country western best. A country band is on the outdoor stage playing as men spin their ladies around on the dancefloor. Katie sits alone watching all the action. Travis Sheppard, the singer of the band, is taking an interest in Katie. She nods her head hello at him. She glances around but does not spot any friendly faces.

Once the band finishes playing a tune, Travis makes his way over to the bar to Katie. Before he can get to her, two women approach Travis and ask for his autograph. He finally makes his way to her.

"Hey, Katie."

"Travis Sheppard, the one and only."

"I'm glad you could come, Katie."

"You didn't think I would?" Katie asks sweetly.

Studying her for a moment, Travis says, "Well, you did say this isn't your type of scene."

"It's definitely not."

"I hope I am?" Travis asks her.

"You might be," Katie says flirting a little.

"I'll be done in an hour. Do you want to meet me at Lucky's Diner? I'm starving." Travis asks.

"Well, since I'm not really sure you'll actually show up... and you're not really sure if I'll show up, either. Let's just say... hopefully we both show up, okay?" Katie says.

"Sounds good to me," Travis says smiling.

"Maybe we'll see each other later," Katie says smiling, as she stands getting ready to leave. Travis gets back to work on stage.

An hour later, Katie walks into Lucky's Diner. She looks around and Travis is nowhere in sight. She is about to turn around and walk out when Travis walks in the door and she turns around right into him.

"Surprise! You're here!" Travis says happily.

"Yea, what a surprise. You're here, too."

Katie slides into the booth and he follows her. They are sitting closely side by side. They stare at each other for a moment. Katie loves the chemistry she feels with him, but she wonders if there is anything more than chemistry between them.

Travis says, "So, you think we should continue having this flaky relationship?"

"I don't know. We're in a relationship?" Katie asks him with a gleam in her eyes. "Why?"

"Because we can always depend on each other...

not to show up?" Travis says teasing her.

They both laugh. They really do enjoy each other's company on the rare occasions they get together.

A waiter shows up to take their order.

"Are you hungry?" Travis asks.

"No, but I'd love a chocolate shake."

"Let me have a double-double with two chocolate shakes... and some fries."

"I'll have that right out," the waiter says to them.

"In all seriousness, Katie. Why don't we take us to another level?"

"Not sure I can handle all the responsibility in that. Can you?"

"I'm willing to find out," Travis says as he kisses her softly on the lips.

"You're always on the road, Travis. It's hard to have a relationship when one person is rarely around."

"Do you want to try?" Travis says fearing the answer.

They look at each other in earnest for a moment. There is some degree of sadness on their faces. There will be no answer to that question tonight.

Katie is deep in thought as she drives home to her rented cottage in Santa Monica. As she pulls into the drive and gets out of her car, she can hear the phone ringing inside. Panic sets in since it is way past midnight, and no news at this hour can be good news. She rushes in the door, drops her shawl and purse, and races to the phone.

"Hello! Katie Baker."

"Katie. It's Mom."

Katie quickly senses the distress in Daisy's voice.

"Mom, what's wrong?"

"Your dad's in the hospital. He's had a mild stroke. He's asking for you. I said I would call."

"Tell him I'm coming home, Mom. I love you. Please tell him I love him, too."

Back in Forgotten, the Champion Estate shines brightly in the early morning sun. Vaqueros are out and about rounding up cattle and tending to the herd. Henry stops by the corrals to check in on the men. Henry is another two decades older now, but his handsome face is still striking. His hair is dark, and it seems time has stood still for him.

Henry now sees his son, Daniel, coming out of the house carrying a suitcase to the truck. Daniel Champion has become a handsome man in his late thirties. The last twenty years have worked out well. He left Forgotten after high school to attend Vanderbilt University in Nashville, Tennessee. After many arguments with his father who insisted he attend Texas A & M to study ranching and agriculture, Daniel prevailed and went to Vanderbilt to study music. Besides, as he had stated to his father many times while debating his position, what was A&M going to teach him that he did not already know about ranching?

While at college, Daniel made some great friends. One in particular, his best friend Byron Scott, had pursued his musical career and had now become a famous country music star.

Daniel had chosen to return to Forgotten after graduation. This morning, Daniel finds himself in another argument with his father. Daniel is traveling to Nashville, and Henry is not too pleased about it.

Byron had given Daniel a call and asked him to come to Nashville for a rehearsal on a new album he was cutting with Daniel's lyrics. He wanted Daniel to sing a duet with him on a single. At first, Daniel was going to refuse Byron's offer, but then decided he needed to get away from the ranch, and it would be great to see Byron and play some music with his old friend.

Henry is yelling at him now, "What the heck are you going to Nashville for?"

"I told you, Dad. I'm going to see my friend Byron and we're going to rehearse a song for his new album."

"When are you going to get serious about taking over this ranch?"

"Dad, I have worked my butt off for you and this ranch most of my life. I think I deserve to get away for a few days."

"Well, you better come back quick," Henry says, knowing he is losing the argument.

Henry has always loathed Daniel's love for music, and he never misses an opportunity to tell him so.

"I told you, Dad. I'll be back in a few days."

Daniel puts his suitcase in his truck and drives away. He is thinking it will be good to get away from his Dad, as well. As he drives down the ranch road, part of him wishes he never had to return to this ranch. But the hill country is in his blood, and he loves this land too much. He realizes he must put up with Henry, since he understands there is no way his father would be able to manage without him.

Hours later, his friend Byron is at Berry Field, the airport in Nashville, waiting to pick him up. He honks at Daniel now as Daniel makes his way over to Byron's truck and gets in.

"Great to see you, brother," Byron says happy to see his old friend.

"I know! It's been awhile."

"Let's grab some lunch and then we'll head to the recording studio."

"Sounds great. Can't wait to see what you've come up with this time!"

"I'm thinking it's going to be a hit!" Byron says excitedly.

"I'm sure it is. You have the magic touch on hit singles!"

They head on down the road as the beautiful city of Nashville lays before them.

CHAPTER 9
Back in Forgotten

Katie arrives the next day at the small hospital in the nearby town of Kerville. She makes her way through the corridors until she finds her dad's hospital room. She places her bag on a chair and goes over to George's bed. He appears to be sleeping peacefully. Almost a sixty-year-old man now, George's hair has grayed some, and his look is more mature and attractive. Katie sits carefully on the edge of the bed and places a tender hand on his cheek. George opens his eyes to see his daughter sitting before him. He swiftly dons a big smile. His little girl has come home to see him.

"Hi, Daddy.

"You came to see your old dad."

"You didn't think I'd let you kick the bucket without saying goodbye first, did you?"

George takes her hand, gives it a kiss, and she leans over to kiss his forehead.

"How are you feeling, Dad?"

"Doc says I'm fine.... Your mom's going to be so happy to see you, Katie. Her friend Mary took her home a while ago to get everything ready for you. She left my truck out front so you could get home."

"The doctor says you need to take it easy, Dad. Mom says you've been working too hard. And the doctor says you have a heart problem. I think we should hire a ranch hand to help you."

"I'm alright. I don't know what all this fuss is about. No help needed. Thank you. And I'm so sorry you had to take time off from work, Katie. I know you've been busy."

"Never too busy for you, Dad. Someone is covering my cases. I won't even be missed. You've had a stroke. The next one could be worse. You could end up having a heart attack. You do need help."

"I don't want nor need any."

"Okay, shush now. Get some rest. The doctor says you can go home tomorrow."

George looks up at his daughter sweetly and says, "I'm glad you're home, Katie."

Katie drives her father's truck from the hospital through Forgotten on the way out to the farm. The town seems smaller and not much has changed. The visits to see her parents over the years have not been as many as she would have liked. She realizes her parents are getting older and need her more than ever. She promises herself she will visit more regularly. She is constantly dismissing her father's requests to move back to Forgotten. Katie cannot imagine how that could ever be possible. How could she trade her exciting life in L.A. to come back to her hometown?

Pulling up to the farmhouse seems surreal this time. She has an odd feeling, as the farm seems empty, simply by knowing her father is not home. He is not there to greet her today. He is in the hospital with a serious condition. How many more times would she get to see him standing there at the front door to welcome her home? Home. She thinks on the word now. Is she home now?

Everything in the house seems dated as Katie walks into the living room. She puts her bags down and looks around, calling up all those deep, wonderful memories. She makes her way to a table where several framed pictures sit.

She picks one up of her, Patrick, and their
parents, of one of the many picnics they had
by the river. Seeing her brother Patrick's silly
face in the photo reminds her of long-ago days
when he was still around. She smiles fondly at
remembering what a clown he was. He always
knew how to make her laugh. Her memories
seem like a dream now. As Katie is deep in
memories, Daisy enters the room. Reading
each other's minds and without words, they
walk toward one another and embrace for a
long moment.

It is a beautiful Texas Hill Country morning.
The sun peaks over the horizon lighting up the
hillsides. A limo pulls up the drive of the
Champion Estate. The driver gets out to open
the passenger's door. Henry Champion has
become more attractive with age as he stands
there now with perfect posture, waiting for his
company to arrive.

Sinclair Davis is a pretty woman in her early
fifties. As she steps out of the limo, Henry
seems surprised. He cannot help noticing her
stunning legs right away. Henry approaches her
and extends a handshake.

"Hello, Ma'am. I'm Henry Champion. And where is Mr. Davis?"

Extending her hand out to Henry, "I'm Sinclair Davis."

"You're the lawyer from Austin that my accountant sent to defend me? Well, I'll be damned."

Sinclair has been through enough of the good old boy network, so she is not intimidated.

"If you prefer a man for the job, I'll hop right back in the car and leave, Mr. Champion. I know this part of the world is still threatened by strong and independent women."

Henry reacts to the way she says the word, 'threatened', but he is not going to let her get the best of him. Besides, he has been checking her out and he likes what he sees.

"Well, my accountant did say you were the best he knows, and you are here, so I'll give you a shot."

"How gracious of you, Mr. Champion."

"You best not blow it," Henry says to her.

Sinclair immediately shoots him a frown clearly showing her distaste in him.

"You can call me Henry."

He escorts her into his estate letting her walk a little ahead of him so he can check out her fabulous legs. Her hips have just the right amount of sway, and he is thinking she better be a good lawyer because he might enjoy having her around.

CHAPTER 10
The Fight Is On

The interior of Mike's Pub on the outskirts of Forgotten is a smoke-filled bar that attracts many of the locals. For such a small town, there are several bars scattered about the town. Mike's Pub is the classiest joint in Forgotten, although none of the furniture matches and there are neon advertising signs everywhere. A pool table sits at the far corner, and a couple of guys are hitting a few balls around.

Daniel Champion is back from Nashville. He and his band are up on the stage playing before a rowdy crowd in Mike's Pub tonight. It is a Friday night, and most of the patrons are out spending some of their paychecks on assorted beverages. A couple of attractive women have their eyes on Daniel, and flirt with him as he performs a country tune. When the band finishes a set, Daniel walks up to the bar to get a cool drink and talk to Mike.

"Give me a Coke, Mike," Daniel asks of the owner.

"You sure I can't get you anything stronger, Daniel?"

"Mike! How long have you known me?"

"Mmmm.... A long time. My whole life, actually," Mike shrugs and responds.

Mike hands Daniel a soda, and Daniel takes a long swig out of it. Just as he is setting it down on the counter, one of the cute women walks up to Daniel.

"Hi, Daniel," Sophie says.

"Hey, how ya' doing," Daniel replies with not a bit of interest in his tone.

"Do you want to get a drink with me after you're done tonight?" Sophie asks.

"Na, thanks. It's been a long day, and I have to be up early to take care of the cattle."

"Well, okay," Sophie says looking as rejected as one can. She gives him an unpleasant look and walks away.

Daniel seems unfazed by the attention.

"I can't believe you, Daniel! Pretty girls throwing themselves at you," Mike says.

"Well, if you're not interested, you're not interested, right?" Daniel replies.

"If you're looking for the perfect woman, you do know she doesn't exist, right?"

Daniel just shakes his head at Mike and laughs.

"I actually thought she did once, Mike. I was so wrong."

Daniel enjoys his soda for another few minutes, and then heads back to the stage to perform.

The Forgotten Courthouse is a busy place this Monday morning. Judge Raye sits on the bench as a courtroom full of people wait their turns to get before the Judge. Henry Champion and his attorney, Sinclair Davis, are seated in the front row as they now listen for the Judge's decision.

With authority, Judge Raye says, "This court's decision is to rule for the defendant, Henry Champion."

It is obvious Henry is delighted by the verdict as he jumps out of his seat. As Sinclair also stands, she is clearly uncomfortable with Henry's overture as he hugs her. He squeezes her tightly as she tries to push him away. Henry is jubilant and flaunts his victory in front of his opponent. The Judge seems indifferent as he heads out. He has seen Henry in action for years, it seems, and he looks the other way.

Sandy Gutierrez, the plaintiff, seems devastated and shoots an evil look toward Henry. Sandy has been in court trying to get back several thousand acres that had once been in her family. Her deed to the land was not able to get validated, and the court has now ruled in Henry's favor.

Henry tips his hat at Sandy and smirks. Sinclair is downright embarrassed by Henry's boastful conduct. Sinclair is not the type of woman to brag and behave in such a fashion. She despises Henry, but also feels a slight attraction to his over the top personality. Or rather, she is attracted to the brazen caricature she finds him to be. Sinclair has known men like this all of her life. Henry is that same shameless type of man and more. He is definitely in a league of his own. She realizes she will have to handle him firmly, or he will roll over her if she allows him. She recognizes that Henry is capable of destroying lives.

George is saying goodbye to the nurse at the hospital in Kerville as Katie assists him from the mandatory wheelchair and into the old Chevy truck. Katie thinks to herself that he does seem a little better today, there is a rosy glow in his cheeks, and that makes her happy. She hopes her dad with take better care of himself going forward.

As Katie hops into the driver's side and pulls away from the hospital, she says, "When are you going to buy a new truck, Dad?"

George sits up a little taller looking a bit hurt.

"What's wrong with my pickup? It's a trusty old friend," George responds while lovingly patting the dashboard. "I hope you're back for good this time, Katie."

"Dad, you know my life is in L.A. My job is there."

"What you wanna live in that hell hole for? Earthquakes, fires, floods, crazy kooks—"

Katie interrupts him, "I like it there."

"Yea, I'll bet."

Katie is not going to get into the same argument with her dad. He has a heart condition, and the last thing she wants to do is upset him. Besides, she knows he is only giving her a hard time because he loves her and would prefer she came back to Forgotten. They ride along in silence for a little bit, but she sees George is not done with the topic.

"We could use a smart attorney in this town. People have to drive all the way to McGovern just to see one," George says.

"Dad, it's 15 miles."

"You remember Andy Cruz?"

"Of course, we did time together in Forgotten High School."

"He's the attorney over in McGovern now."

"Yea, I heard."

"Why don't you drop by and say hello to him? I'm sure he would love to know you're in town." With a little wink he adds, "He's single."

"Oh my gosh, Dad. Every time I'm in town, you're trying to set me up!"

George is going to give it one last shot, shifting position to face her more.

"Stay for good this time, Katie."

"Dad. I will stay for a little while. Until you get better and I find you some help."

"Like I've said a million times to you and your mother. I do not need any help. I can manage."

As they drive a little longer, they come upon a funeral procession. They stop on the side of the road to wait for the vehicles as they slowly pass. George removes his hat out of respect.

"Who's funeral, Dad?" Katie asks.

"Mrs. Gutierrez. Sandy's mom," George replies.

"Oh, no. So sad. Look at all the vehicles. Must be hundreds of them. Wow!" Katie remarks.

"She was a lovely lady, loved by so many. She will be greatly missed in this town. Her daughter, Sandy, just lost her court case against Henry." George adds.

Katie is curious about that but does not feel like talking about Henry right now.

"They say the length of a funeral procession says a lot about how loved and respected you were when you were alive," Katie says.

"That is definitely true," George agrees.

Ten minutes later, the procession finally goes past, and George and Katie continue on their way home again.

The next day, Sheriff Pete's office is crowded with townspeople. Sandy Gutierrez, Mr. Lozano, Mr. Felder, and others are all trying to speak at once with angry or concerned voices. Sheriff Pete has gotten a bit older, and his hair is looking a little grayer and thinner these days. He is still the kind-hearted man the town knows and loves.

"Alright, one at a time," Sheriff Pete says. "I can't hear all of you at once. Go ahead, Lozano. You go first."

"My father once owned this piece of land," Mr. Lozano says, while holding up a deed in his hand. "This is the original deed to our land, and we want our property back."

Sheriff Pete says, "Let me guess, Champion's land now, also?"

"Yes," Mr. Lozano replies.

"Just like me," Sandy says agreeing with Mr. Lozano.

Sheriff Pete looks at Sandy, "You're ready to face off with him again, Sandy?"

"We can't quit, Pete," Sandy says with determination. "We have to get our lands back."

"Okay, folks. Tell you what. Katie Baker is in town and I hear she is a darn good lawyer. How about we go talk to her tomorrow. She'll know what you need to do," Sheriff Pete says with an assuring tone.

The townspeople look at one another, nodding, and mumbling in agreement.

CHAPTER 11
The Reunion

Katie makes her way down to the river's edge. A late summer breeze blows on her face. She saunters about, with her mind on her childhood. She recalls playing and swimming in the river with her brother, Patrick. She has missed him so much over these past 20 years. She sits on the river's edge now, gazing out over the river. Her mind deep in thought and lost in memories.

"Hello, Katie."

Katie turns around to see Daniel Champion sitting up high on his horse. His Stetson rests back on his head, his shirt is opened a bit revealing some of his chest. Their eyes meet for a moment. Katie has not seen Daniel in twenty years, since that unforgettable dreadful night, and she is taken aback at how handsome and sexy of a man he has become. She thinks to herself it is a bit startling to see him all grown up like this.

Daniel continues, "Heard you were back."

Katie does not respond.

"I hope that your Dad is feeling better," Daniel says, obviously struggling with her indifference.

Katie refuses to look at him again. Instead, she looks out over the river, hoping he will soon leave.

Daniel dismounts, approaches a bit, but still remains a distance away.

"Well, it's good to see you, Katie. You look gorgeous!"

Katie rises and walks away. Daniel is visibly hating this.

"You stay pretty well hid when you're in town. I heard you came in six months ago for your mom's birthday," Daniel adds, letting her silence ride. He is thinking about leaving but ambles a few steps toward her.

"I have no interest in talking to you, Daniel. Please leave."

"Uhhh... this is Champion property, remember?" Daniel says trying to maintain his cool.

"Correction—Your family stole this land from my dad's family many years ago," Katie responds angrily.

Daniel's face sours and he looks like he has

been punched in the gut. Katie merely glares at him for a few seconds. Daniel has heard all rumors for years, and has yet to challenge his father about it, fearing the discovery of the truth. Daniel remains stunned as Katie walks off.

The Baker's crop fields extend out for more than a thousand acres. George is about to climb up onto his old tractor when Katie comes up behind him wearing a work shirt, blue jeans, and boots.

"And just what the heck do you think you're going to do, mister?"

"Aww, Katie," George says wincing, he has been caught.

"Mom says you're a stubborn fool, and she's right. No work for you today, or any time soon for that matter."

"This man has work to do, sweetie," George says, while obliging her request.

"It hasn't been a week since you got out of the hospital, Dad. You know what Doc said."

"Aww, Katie. You're just like your Mom. Relentless!"

"Please Dad, you need to rest. You need a break."

Katie snatches George's old cowboy hat off his head, puts it on, jumps into the tractor, and starts it up.

Father and daughter exchange a look, then she motors off to work the field. George watches after her with some resignation and pride.

"I'm so proud of you, daughter," George mutters to himself under his breath. "I taught you well."

The sun is setting over the horizon on the cotton fields as Katie comes driving back. They shine like snow in the distance behind her. She is silhouetted against the western sky as she heads for the barn. She parks it, hops down, and heads for the farmhouse. As she goes, she wipes perspiration from her brow with her shirt sleeve, just like she has seen her father do so many times. Katie laughs at her action and memory.

"Like father, like daughter," she thinks to herself grinning.

As she comes around to the front of the farmhouse, Katie notices several vehicles. She comes through the front door and stops, waiting for people to jump out and yell 'surprise' as if she has just caught them throwing her a party. Looking around, she senses quickly this is not a celebration by the glum looks on their faces. Gathered in the living room she sees people she has not seen in some time. Sheriff Pete is there, as is Mr. Lozano, Sandy Gutierrez, Mr. Felder, and a few others she cannot quite remember. Daisy runs around giving the guests a glass of her famous lemonade, and George sits quietly observing it all.

"Hi, Katie," Sheriff Pete speaks first. "Welcome home. Good to see you back in Forgotten."

"Hi, folks! Hi, Sheriff!" Katie says, as she gives Sheriff Pete a hug and a kiss on the cheek.

"These people have come to talk to you, Katie," her dad says to her.

Mr. Lozano adds, "I hope you don't mind us coming out to see you, Katie."

Daisy hands a glass of lemonade to Katie.

"Katie, the folks have come out here to talk to you about land deeds they have to the properties their families once owned," Daisy says in a calming voice.

Katie has a big sip of lemonade, says nothing, letting the people speak. Though she is not surprised by their claims, she is interested in the fact that they are all coming forward at this time.

Mr. Lozano comes a little closer and says to Katie, "Sheriff says you know a way to get our land back from Champion."

Katie shoots Sheriff Pete a look, as he treads water and says, "Well, I only said---"

George cuts in, "They have deeds to property over on Champion land."

"We want a chance to get our lands back, Katie," Mr. Felder jumps in.

"I want what my family has a right to have," Sandy says.

Sheriff Pete adds, "I'd like to see Henry get

what's coming to him just like anybody. But Sandy, you just lost your mom and the case against Henry. Can you deal with another loss right now?"

"And Henry does have the money to hire the best lawyers," George pipes in.

Sandy says earnestly, "I have to do this for my family. I must get my family's land back."

Katie says in a hopeful tone, "I think we have enough folks to bring a lawsuit against Champion."

Katie looks at them all. They seem sincere, but she also knows their daily situations.

Katie says, "I've known most of you all of my life. Some of you work for your living on what is considered 'Champion' land. You all have to understand the risk you'd be taking, because we all know Henry can make your lives a living hell."

"But we have to try," Mr. Felder responds.

"Even though justice is served in a court of law, there's always a loser. It could be you. And that could be worse than what you're all dealing with right now," Katie says while looking at each of them.

There is a heavy silence as they all look at one another.

"Henry's a powerful man. Katie's right. It's a big risk," Daisy adds.

"Look, I'll go see Andy Cruz in McGovern tomorrow. I'm board certified in Texas. I was involved in a similar lawsuit up in Dallas a few years back," Katie tells them.

"Did you win?" Sandy asks.

"Actually, no," Katie responds.

Everyone in the room moans.

"Listen, we'll look into the ramifications of filing a multi-plaintiff lawsuit against Champion," Katie says.

"What's that, Katie?" Mr. Felder asks.

"That's when everyone gets to point a finger at the same time," Katie says in a silly voice.

Katie sends them all a hopeful smile. They all seem satisfied.

She turns to her dad and says, "Will that old truck of yours make it thirty miles at one time?"

Everybody laughs. You know it is a touchy subject for George. He loves his truck. Everyone in town knows he will do whatever it takes to keep his old truck friend running.

"You're kidding, right?" is George's only response.

It is a beautiful day in the quiet nearby hill country town of McGovern as Katie drives in. She heads straight to Main Street, looking for Andy's law office. The town square features a beautiful red brick courthouse in the renaissance style architecture and is considered to be among the top architectural masterpieces in Texas. Cute shops and businesses line the streets which surround the courthouse.

Katie sees Andy's business sign and pulls into a parking spot and gets out. As she walks away, George's old truck spits and coughs at her, and finally backfires! Katie is startled as she jumps and chuckles and heads into the building. Katie walks into Andy's office and he stands quickly to hug her. He is nicely dressed in Texas hill country professional attire of blue jeans, starched shirt, sport coat, and no tie. And of course, he is sporting some nice, expensive Lucchese cowboy boots.

Greeting her happily, "It's been one helluva long time. You look as beautiful as ever, counselor."

"Thanks, Andy! So great to see you. You're looking fine yourself!"

They look at each other with big smiles for a few moments, and then Andy realizes he still has a hold of Katie's hand.

"Come sit down. By your phone call, it seems you've taken a dive into some pretty deep water," Andy says taking a seat next to Katie.

"Yep! You could definitely say that!"

Katie takes a quick glance around his office. It is neatly organized and shows Andy's good taste. She quickly notes that it appears Andy has done well for himself all these years.

"I don't know how this is going to turn out for these families," Andy says to her.

"Henry's a dangerous person to be messing with, that's for sure."

"Have you had lunch, Katie? Let's go grab a bite. Do you remember in high school when we all used to drive into McGovern to go to Molly's? If you can believe it, she's still here... and she still cooks up a mean chicken fried steak. We can talk about everything over lunch."

CHAPTER 12
Henry

Several vaqueros are hanging out at the
Champion corrals enjoying their lunch. Soon, it
is time for them to get back to work. Henry
rides up on horseback, bringing in a calf. Henry
dismounts, heading over to the chuck wagon for
a cup of coffee. The cook hands Henry a cup
just as Daniel rides up and dismounts.

"Hey, Dad!" Daniel says to him. "You sure ride
pretty for an old vaquero who's got one foot in
the grave."

"I can ride circles around anyone, anytime,"
Henry brags. "And who you 'callin old?"

One of Henry's workers, Willy Watson, says
to Henry kissing up to him, "Everyone knows
you're the best vaquero in these parts, Jefe."

"Damn right!" Henry says.

"Modest, too," Daniel says mocking him.

Some of the ranch hands snort at the humor.

"Now, John Champion, my grandfather, there
was a great vaquero!" Henry says proudly,
looking about the land.

"John Champion started this spread with seventy acres he won in a poker game.... Now it's hundreds of thousands, one of the biggest in Texas," Henry says proudly. "You oughta be proud of who you are, Danny, mighty proud."

Daniel just looks at him with some displeasure. He has heard the talk behind his father's back for years.

"You need to give up that music business of yours and get more serious about running this ranch. I won't live forever, you know," Henry says admonishing Daniel.

Daniel gives his father a half-hearted nod and then shakes his head. Henry has taken every opportunity to criticize Daniel for his music for years. Daniel's choice of a hobby is a matter of embarrassment to Henry, it seems. Henry and Daniel see a pickup truck approaching the estate. They walk over to the long drive as Andy Cruz pulls up.

"Hello, Daniel. Henry," Andy says, as he walks up to them.

Andy Cruz wastes no time and hands Henry an envelope, "Let it be known you've been served, Mr. Champion."

With that, Andy gets in his pickup and drives away. He leaves both Champions with looks of confusion on their faces. Henry quickly scans the contents of the envelope and disgustedly crumples up the notice. He pitches it on the dirt and walks away.

"What is that all about, Dad?" Daniel asks while picking up the paperwork and following his dad into the house.

"Ungrateful sons of bitches! They'll never get away with it," Henry says angrily.

"Get away with what, Dad?"

"You call that lady lawyer in Austin and tell her to get her butt down here right away," Henry orders.

"Your attorney?"

"Don't question me, boy. Just do it."

"Don't call me a boy, Dad. What's going on?"

Henry spits out a nervous chuckle and says, "Oh-ho, you'll know soon enough."

Andy Cruz has a lot of people from Forgotten in his office today. He and Katie are patiently listening to a gathering of folks, some of whom are angry about the pending lawsuit, others who support it. It seems the word has gotten around, and now other deed owners are wanting to get on board.

One protestor says, "Champion's got most of the land and jobs. Either way, I'm gonna lose."

"You lose this lawsuit, Andy, some of us ain't gonna have jobs. Hell, that crazy man could fire us right now for this. How are we supposed to feed our kids?"

Andy responds, "I understand that. I can only tell you that based on all the evidence so far, it seems Katie and I have a good case."

"It's time the Champion name got what's due. They've been terrorizin' folks in the hill country for generations," Cooper says.

"Katie, some of us don't have deeds, and if our families ever did, they got lost or stolen. We're the ones who are gonna pay."

Mr. Lozano says to them, "If my deed stands up, I'll have four thousand acres. I can't work all the land by myself. That goes for Ortiz, Cooper, Alex, all of us. I for one would be willing to sell some of it... or offer permanent work so you could afford to buy. It can be worked out."

Felder says, "Antonio's right. We haven't been able to buy any land around here, 'cause there's been none around here to buy."

"It's all Champions, and this is our chance to make it rightfully ours again," Sandy says.

"I'm just one man. What's my guarantee," one of the men protesting says.

"That's why we're all in this together, Benny," Mr. Lozano says.

"Look everyone, Andy and I aren't making any promises. But you do have justice on your side," Katie says to them.

Benny says, "Okay, Katie. Andy. I'll keep an open mind about this even though we're up against a horse's ass like Henry—bless him, he pays me every week!"

After his remark, he lets out a hilarious chuckle, and quickly the laughter is contagious.

The downtown Austin skyline sparkles as the lake below glistens in the sunshine. Henry and Daniel sit patiently in Sinclair's office waiting for her to get off the phone. Sinclair's office is located in a beautiful suite overlooking the state capitol building. It is quite an impressive office with floor to ceiling and wall to wall windows on two sides of the room. The office also faces the breathtaking scenery and the lake below. By the exquisite furnishes, it is obvious Sinclair has great taste. There are pale colors in the upholstery and rich brown wood furniture in walnut, featuring a desk, credenza, sideboard, and chairs. Henry is looking around with a long worried look on his face. Daniel seems indifferent about what is happening. Finally, Sinclair gets off the phone.

"So sorry to keep you waiting, gentlemen. And I'm sorry I couldn't come see you at the ranch, Henry. Thank you for making the trip up here."

Henry gets right to the point. "So... what am I gonna do about all these people, Sinclair?"

Henry cannot help noticing Sinclair's lovely figure as she walks to pour herself a glass of water from the sideboard. She offers a glass of water to Henry and Daniel.

"I've had an expert check out the deeds, Henry. They appear legit. We still need them validated, but so far, it looks like you're in a bit of trouble."

"I'm not losing what's taken my family generations to build. Take care of it."

"You could offer the plaintiffs an out of court compensatory settlement, and squash the suit," Sinclair says.

"Whose side are you on?" Henry asks.

"Well at this very moment, mine. Dismantling this thing one family at a time might be the only way," Sinclair says in a positive tone.

Henry's listening. The gears are grinding behind his wicked eyes, as he says, "You may have something there, honey. I could start with that Baker tramp herself. She's the one who started this crap."

Daniel does not care for the reference about

Katie, and tries not to interfere, but he cannot help himself.

"Watch your mouth, Dad."

"That's right, Henry. Please show some respect for me and my office. Hold your foul tongue."

Henry's surprised by Sinclair's guts, as not many women have stood up to him in the past.

Sinclair continues, "Katie's a sharp attorney. I've checked her record."

"What about that dimwitted Cruz kid?" Henry asks.

"Henry, hate to break it to you. But the last thing you can call Andy Cruz is stupid. Andy's a real tough attorney. He's well-known to be a really smart and fair guy in trials. He hasn't sold his integrity nor office to anyone. Perhaps he and Ms. Baker can speak to the families about settling this thing."

Henry's face is clouded with fear and apprehension. There is no way he is going down without a fight.

It has been a couple of weeks since George was in the hospital, and he is looking healthier and stronger these days. He is quite the attractive man, and the rest he has had away from work looks good on him. He mounts his horse and takes a ride down the road away from his farmhouse to check on some of the fences and cross fences. Along the road comes a new vehicle he does not recognize.

George sees Henry driving. Both men stop -- meeting each other head-on. George stands his horse before Henry's vehicle, not allowing Henry to continue on his way.

"Get your truck out of my way and off my land, Champion."

"It's not a truck, George. It's a brand-new damn Suburban! Like it?" Henry replies with arrogance.

"I don't care what it is, Henry. Back it up and get out of here."

George pulls the shotgun out of its saddle sleeve and cocks it. Henry's smile fades a bit.

"Back it outta here, or it'll be a brand-new damn Suburban with holes in it."

"Now Georgie, I just want to talk to Katie about the court case. If she pursues this thing, it will cost you."

Daisy is now on the front porch and overhears Henry threatening George. BAM! George fires a single shot into one of Henry's fenders. Henry is stunned! He cannot actually believe George is capable of doing such a thing.

"What the hell you doing, Baker?! I just want to patch things up!" Henry fumes!

"Patch it with bondo!" George yells at him as Henry throws the Suburban into reverse and beats it out of there.

"How's that for you, Daisy?" George mutters under his breath.

George chuckles watching Henry drive away. Daisy just shakes her head angrily and then grits her teeth but looks at George with reserved pride.

CHAPTER 13
Daniel

Katie always loved sitting on the front porch of the farmhouse watching the rain fall. Tonight, the rain is coming down hard as Katie, George, and Daisy sit on the porch enjoying the rain and cooler temperature.

"I sure miss the smell of rain," Katie says to her folks.

"I'll bet. You probably don't get much rain in Los Angeles," Daisy responds.

"Rarely, unless it's a flooding rain. Boy, it's really coming down!"

"Like my Pa used to say, you ain't seen it rain 'till the cow patties float," George says with a twang.

"How poetic, honey," Daisy says laughing at him.

Katie and Daisy smile at him as the rain falls steadily.

"I saw Daniel at the river," Katie says surprising both Daisy and George.

George is about to say something, pauses, gazes at the rain instead.

A few moments later, "He took my advice. He's never been back here," George says to Katie.

"You've been too hard on the boy, George. He's paid dearly for what happened to Patrick," Daisy says softly. "I can't imagine the guilt he's been living with since."

"Dad. Promise me you'll stay out of Henry's way. This lawsuit could push that crazy nut to the brink."

"I ain't gonna hide from the man, Katie. I aint' gonna hide."

Katie frowns, and George stands and plants a kiss on her cheek.

"I don't want you getting hurt," Daisy says to him.

"How about I fix us some thick, juicy, pan-fried steaks?" Katie offers.

"Has your cooking improved any?" George teases. "I remember the last time I had to eat one of your steaks. I didn't know if I should eat it or bury it."

"Dad!" Katie shrieks.

George is laughing at her now. Daisy shakes her head at him.

"Hey, it's not my fault Mom never let me cook around here."

Looking straight at her mom and mimicking her Mom's voice she continues, "It's my kitchen, everybody out."

"Yea, well. Okay," Daisy says in a guilty voice.

George says sitting back down, "Alright then, make mine---"

"I know, Dad. Medium rare," Katie says interrupting, as she stands and heads inside.

George and Daisy give one another a funny gaze, and then there is a clap of thunder and they both jump out of their chairs and quickly run inside.

The Lozano's are owners of Forgotten's one of only two grocery stores in town. Mr. Lozano is at the cash register as Daniel Champion enters the store with an angry attitude.

"Hey, Daniel," Mr. Lozano says as Daniel walks through the door.

"How can you turn against my father like this?"

Mr. Lozano is caught off guard by Daniel's anger.

"Danny, we're not---"

Cutting him off Daniel says, "After all my father's done for you and your family. Who bailed you out when you damn near lost this store?"

Mrs. Lozano hears the arguing and comes out from the back of the store and joins her husband in the conversation.

"Daniel, we don't want to hurt you," she says.

"We just want back what rightfully and legally belongs to our family," Mr. Lozano says kindly to Daniel.

"Why is it that everyone in this town hates my father until the moment they want something from him?" Daniel says and storms out.

An expert in land deed authentication is sitting in Andy Cruz's office studying the paperwork before him.

"What do you think, Pablo? We have a shot?"

"I've seen the real thing, and the bogus deeds that look fairly authentic. I can unquestionably tell the difference."

"Well, you're the expert. Are these real? Are they going to fly?" Andy asks.

"I guarantee you, Andy. I'm going to find out. More and more folks are bringing in their deeds for me to look at. This thing is getting out of control."

The next day, Katie is sitting by the river when Daniel rides up. He dismounts and walks over to her... She rises to leave.

"What do you want, Daniel? Please leave me alone."

"You're the most unforgiving..." He is going to say something he will probably regret later, so he does not finish his sentence.

As Daniel gets closer, Katie moves away.

"You Champions continue to ruin lives. Henry's made Dad suffer all these years. And it's your fault my brother is gone," Katie says unloading on him.

"You know it was an accident. I haven't touched a drop of alcohol since that night. Just the smell of it, makes me sick... makes me remember."

The pain in Daniel's voice, makes Katie turn to look at him. She has wanted to forgive him but has not found the way.

"I know Daisy, George... And you... have suffered for it. God knows I have. I want to change what happened, but I can't, Katie."

Daniel sees Katie looking at him less indignantly.

Daniel continues, "I miss Patrick. He was my best friend. And I miss the little girl who sang with me in the river and who laughed at everything I'd say. The little girl who once lost her bathing suit top in the river."

He walks closer, but stops as Katie says, "Save it, Daniel. I'm not interested in your fantasies."

"I guess the Katie I knew is gone. The Katie I see before me now is a stranger, a mean cold hearted !"

They overlap as Katie finishes his sentence, "A chip off the old daddy block aren't you, Champ?"

This really gets to Daniel as his expression sours, and Katie knew it would.

"I'm not like Henry. He isn't my real father. You know I'm nothing like him."

Katie responds sarcastically, "What happened to the Champion pride?"

Their connecting gaze is powerful, and it begins to soften. He grabs her to him and kisses her hard. At first, she resists, but she kisses him back with a long passionate kiss. Then she pulls away. Daniel breathes a deep sigh, turns, and heads toward his horse.

As he is about to ride away, he says, "Let go of

it, Katie. I'm angry, too. You're not the only one who's hurting. I wish I could change the past. But I can't."

Shaken and confused, Katie looks after him as he rides away.

George is at the Livestock Auction today. The same auctioneer is still there rattling away all these many years later. As he chatters off another sale, the ranchers and farmers bid on their picks. George sits alone amid the crowd awaiting his pick to come up. Henry walks over to him and sits down next to him.

"You don't have your shotgun, so I guess you won't be shooting at me, George."

"Can't you leave me the hell alone?"

"I don't want to lose my land, George."

"It's never been yours to lose."

"I'll fight to keep what's mine. They say desperate men are capable of anything. They will do crazy things," Henry says in a threatening voice.

"Nothing you've ever done has been sane, Henry."

"Listen ol'poke. A lot of folks don't like what's going on. I wouldn't want to see your sweet daughter of yours getting hurt."

George stands and grabs Henry's collar with two hands. Some of the folks present gossip and snicker at this encounter.

"Calm down, George. You know this stress thing isn't good for your ticker. Can't have you croaking on me. Shit, folks will say I killed you."

"Ever threaten my daughter, and you'll regret it," George says pulling on his shirt as he grabs harder.

George lets him loose, and Henry conveys the usual smirk at him. George's face is a bright red, and he looks angrier than ever.

"You stay the hell away from my family or I'll hunt you down like an animal," George says, really trying to sound persuasive.

Henry focuses his attention back to the auctioneer. He is grinning from ear to ear, as

George leaves him to conduct his business as usual. Henry seems unfazed, as George trembles with adrenaline as he walks out of the auction building.

Sometime later, Katie is on her way out of Andy Cruz's office. She heads for the old Chevy and as she hops in, she notices a note stuck on the steering wheel that simply reads, 'Quit.' A dead bird is lying on the floorboard of the truck.

Out at the Champion Estate, Elena is busy cleaning as Daniel comes through the front door. The phone rings as he makes his way through the house to answer it. Elena tries to answer, but Daniel waves her off.

"I'll get it, Elena. Champion Ranch," Daniel says as he picks up the phone.

Katie is on the other end and says, "Tell Henry to back off! His childish threats and immature antics won't make a difference this time."

"Katie?" Daniel responds surprised. "What's going on?"

Dial tone. Daniel is puzzled, and slams down the receiver.

Daniel walks into the Library where his father is enjoying a drink in the middle of the day.

"What the hell are you doing," Daniel asks his father.

Henry nearly chokes, starts coughing, at being started by Daniel's presence.

Daniel sees the booze in his father's hand and swipes the glass away from him, placing it on a table hard, spilling some.

"You're nothing but a stinking drunk! I'm glad we're not related," Daniel yells at him.

Henry is still coughing as he chokes out, "Daniel! What's gotten into you?"

Daniel starts to leave and says, "I'm sick of your crap!"

"Can I say something here, Daniel?"

Daniel turns and glares at him. He decides to let his father talk. Henry might say something to implicate himself that he will regret saying later.

"First, I oughta kick your ass for disrespecting me like this. What the hell's the matter with you?" Henry says finally collecting his breath.

"You threatened Katie."

"I assure you, Danny. I have nothing to do with any threats against Katie."

"Don't you go near her... Or George or Daisy. And keep Johnny Spader and Willy Watson away from them, too. Or I swear, I'll hurt those assholes real good."

Henry has a funny look on his face as he approaches Daniel. He sizes up his son, trying to get the best of him and get Daniel to react.

"Shit boy, you're still soft for the girl, ain't ya?" Henry says mockingly. "You've missed out on some real respectable girls. Hell, you could've married that Harper girl from Kerville, comes from damn good stock."

"You mean she comes from damn good money, don't you, Dad?"

"What the hell's wrong with having money? You say it like it's sinful to be rich. I ain't seen you bitchin' about money these last thirty-nine years."

Looking out of the window at his vast spread of land, Henry adds, "If you combined all the land she'd inherit one day, together with Champion land, you'd have the biggest spread in the state of Texas."

"Money and power are all that matter to you," Daniel says with disgust.

"It is all that matters. You're just like your mother, Olivia. You act self-righteous about money. But enjoy having it all the same."

"You never speak of my mother. It's as if she never existed. Why is that, Dad?"

"When you were a boy, you became sad when I mentioned her, so I quit talking about her."

"And you've never spoken of your father, Frank. Why?"

"He died when I was around twelve. I don't remember much about him anymore."

Daniel is looking at him with anger showing on his face. He has heard the rumors.

"So, what's your problem, Daniel?"

"Are what people saying true?"

"What's that?" Henry asks as if he could care less about the question.

Daniel is now standing before the painting of his great-grandfather.

"Did your grandfather, John Champion, steal and kill for the land around here?"

Moments of silence, and Daniel seethes as Henry ignores him. Henry gets another glass and pours himself another drink.

Daniel continues, "Answer me, Father."

Henry says," The Champions have always been king around these parts, son. It takes an iron fist to rule them. If you don't handle them tight, they'll walk all over you. You should know that by now."

"You're not answering me. These people have deeds, Dad. From what I hear, they seem legit."

Henry laughs and says, "They're phony. They'll never stand up in court. Just like the last one. This is Champion land and always will be. That music of yours is never going to pay like this here land and ranch will."

Silence fills the room for a few moments. Daniel waits for Henry to speak again.

"Well, that answers it," Daniel says getting in Henry's face. "One more time. Leave Katie and her family the hell alone."

Daniel takes a few steps, puts on his hat, looks back at his father, and then calmly walks away.

CHAPTER 14
He Is At It Again

The men are celebrating the end of the work week in Sally's Saloon tonight. Of course, as usual, the place is packed, and the mob is in full-on drinking mode. A Mexican singer plays his guitar and sings some ballads in Spanish in a corner of the bar. The men are hollering, drinking, and carrying on. Here comes sweet Sally with a round of drinks, flirting with all the men, as they order more drinks from her. She is at the bar again pouring drafts and enjoying her bustling business.

"Well, one's my limit," Felder says, as he gets up to leave. "I'm not blowing my whole paycheck in one night. My wife will kill me!"

He exits, as Henry Champion walks in. Henry's men, Willy Watson and Johnny Spader, are in tow.

"Hiya, Henry!" Sally exclaims loudly calling out to him.

Henry laughs, grabbing Sally around the waist spinning her around. Sally does her dancing best to keep up, laughing with him.

"Give me some of your finest, Sally!"

"Always the best for you, Henry!" Sally squeals with delight, Henry being one of her best customers.

Sally makes a beeline around the bar and pours Henry's drink. Henry scans the premises and finds a place at the bar and sits down.

Sally sets down a shot of whiskey in front of him.

Henry takes it, raises it in the air and says, "Evening, boys! A mighty fine establishment to spend your paychecks in. To your—"

Henry knocks the glass over as he sets it down.

"Do-er again, Sally," Henry says shouting at her.

It is obvious Henry has already had a few too many to drink as he sways on the bar stool. He gazes about the room taking inventory of the men present. The crowd is beginning to feel uneasy at Henry's attention. It is plain that when Henry walked in, the party ended, even though the musician continues to play. Other than the sound of the music, no one is talking.

Henry's face is beginning to turn evil as he says to them, "Most of you men have been with me a long time. I appreciate your loyalty. Some of you... have decided to turn against me."

Henry is looking at the faces of the men with disdain, as he becomes more belligerent. The singer stops playing.

"Ya'll know who you are! You're fired! If I catch any of you near the ranch, I'll shoot you for trespassing."

A near drunk ranch hand stands and goes for Henry and says, "You son of a b-!"

He is stopped by Henry's men who proceed to beat the heck out of him and then toss him to the floor. They seem to be enjoying themselves as they inflict pain on the man. The other men in the bar look away and get back to their business, not wanting to get involved. They do not want to meet Henry's gaze as he glares around the room.

"You've been warned," Henry says to them while heading for the door.

"We're happy to take care of any of you anytime," Willy Watson says.

"Night, Sally," Henry says as he puts on his hat and tips it at her.

Henry and his men walk out without paying.

"Put it on his tab, Ed," Sally mutters under her breath loud enough for her bartender to hear.

The Champion Estate is dark, as Henry is lying in bed in a drunken stupor and obviously passed out.

He is having another nightmare and painfully yells, "Olivia... Olivia! Daisy!"

Henry's eyes open wide as the darkness of his room surrounds him, the whites of his eyes clouded in pain and barely visible in the dark. Henry is having a memory of his childhood. He is a boy again and hears and sees what is happening in his mind's eye.

He sees his grandfather, John Champion, looking down at him saying with satisfaction, "Your Pa is dead. He's had an unfortunate accident. You're all mine to raise now."

A young Henry looks up in fear at the frightening and distorted face of his grandfather. Henry yells and is now wide awake and sitting straight up in his bed. Tears flow down his miserable and beaten face.

A full moon is burning brightly over the Texas countryside. George is out for a walk this late evening. He looks over the farm he loves so dearly, and says to himself, "You've been patient for fifty years."

Katie catches up to her father. "Pretty moon. Nice night, Dad!"

She takes his arm, and they gaze out over the countryside now beautifully lit by the moon's blue light.

After a few moments, George says, "Folks around here have always been afraid of the full moon."

Katie looks up to him, wondering where he is headed with this.

George continues, "People were burned as they slept in their beds or shot trying to escape their burning homes during the night."

A coyote howls in the distance.

"Dad, why are you talking about this?"

"There's a saying, Katie. Dogs once scalded are even afraid of cold water. Well, this old dog's been afraid far too long."

Katie is beginning to understand the reference and says, "Dad. Please be careful. I don't trust Henry. He's dangerous and crazy. I don't want you to get hurt."

"Thank you, sweetie. I'll be okay."

"I was thinking of heading back to L.A. But I don't think I should leave before the trial, and we still need to find you some help."

"Deep down you know this is where you belong, Katie."

"C'mon, let's get inside," Katie responds, before her dad starts going down that road.

Katie puts her arm around her dad's waist, and they head on back to the farmhouse.

Back at the Champion Estate that same night, Dr. Manning is standing by Henry's bed examining him. Daniel is standing near the door, his arms crossed in disgust.

"I can't keep coming out here in the middle of the night, Henry. You have to stop drinking. You've got yourself one heck of a heart problem. The alcohol is going to kill you," Dr. Manning says.

"I'm fine," Henry replies, trying to act tough, and acting completely differently than when he woke up from his nightmare earlier.

"You're not fine, Dad. You need to take better care of yourself."

"See that he gets some rest. I'll check up on him in the morning," Doctor Manning says to Daniel.

"I'm sorry to bring you out here in the middle of the night again," Daniel says to the doctor.

"It's alright, Daniel. Call me if you need me. You know I don't make house calls for just anybody."

To Henry, "Please stop the drinking. Tonight, it was hyperventilation, the next time you could have a heart attack from all the stress."

CHAPTER 15
Secrets

Henry's attorney, Sinclair Davis, is driving to
Forgotten to meet with Henry to prepare him for
the trial. She is dressed to the nines as she
cruises down the highway in her shiny, brand
new 1976 Lincoln Continental. She is lost.
She has driven for miles and miles, and there
has been nowhere to stop to get directions. She
finally comes upon an old gas station on the
side of the highway. She lowers her window as
she pulls up to the pump. An elderly man sits
in a chair but does not stand up to greet her. A
teenage boy pokes his head out of the gas
station to see if he needs to get busy and pump
some gas.

"Morning, Miss," the elderly man says to her.

"Good morning, Sir. I'm so lost. Could you
please tell me how to get to Forgotten?"

"Let's see. Take highway 128 here about 10
miles. Then turn left and take 16 South.
If you pass the dairy, you've gone too far. Yep,
16 South.... It'll take you right into Forgotten."

"Thank you!" Sinclair says as she drives away.

"Have a safe drive," the man replies.

George sits at the kitchen table and pours himself a glass of lemonade from the fresh batch Daisy just made. He hears his pickup approaching as Daisy is peering out of the kitchen window. As the pickup pulls up into the driveway, Katie hops out. She enters the house and goes into the kitchen, dropping her shoulder bag and a folder on the table. Katie sighs and sits next to George. Daisy comes over and joins them. Daisy pours a glass of lemonade and hands it to Katie.

"Thanks, Mom."

George notices something is on Katie's mind. She is wearing that *all business look* he has come to know well by now.

"So, what's going on, Katie," George asks.

"I know John Champion stole your father's land. Patrick George Baker purchased the piece of land by the river with the stone fireplace in 1910."

George shoots a suspicious look at Katie.

She hands her father the folder. He grabs it, not seeming to care enough to look inside.

"It's an article I found in the Forgotten Newspaper dated April 24, 1910. It lists some of the new residents and other local news bits," Katie adds.

George seems satisfied, "There you are then."

"Dad, it's not a deed, just a newspaper article. It won't stand up in court."

George seems a bit disappointed, but not much.

"So, where's the deed to your Daddy's land?"

"Haven't seen it in a very long time," George responds.

"I will handle this, Dad. I am not going to let you testify against that man. Doctor said no stress."

"That's right, George. I want you to stay away from Henry," Daisy pipes in.

"Aww, Daisy. All of my life I put up with the humiliation and cruelty from Henry. I disappointed you 'cause I was never a man for a fight. My way of doing nothing was the way I kept my family safe. My Pa stood up to John Champion – and it cost him and his family their lives.

Katie shoots him a surprised look, actually a bit stunned to hear him finally speak of it. She has heard the rumors, but never a word from George about this before now.

"This is my chance to set things straight for my Pa, my Ma, and my brother and sisters.
I'm going to testify if it's the last thing I do on this earth!" George says with unexpected valor.

"No, Mom's right. We can't let you do this, Dad. Henry hates you, and there's no telling what he might do."

"I don't want to go through the rest of my life without you, George," pleads Daisy.

George looks at them both. Sees he is outnumbered, shrugs, and leaves the room.

Back at the Champion Estate, Sinclair Davis has arrived and is getting comfortable. She and Henry are relaxing outside on the terrace.

Sinclair is fanning herself with a newspaper from the late summer heat. She is enjoying a glass of iced tea, but one never knows what Henry is drinking.

"You do have all the deeds to all of your land, don't you, Henry?" Sinclair asks him firmly.

Henry does not respond.

"Henry, I've told you before. We need all the documents in order before the trial."

Henry remains silent, and a then a realization and a frightened gaze moves over his face.

"I've got news for you, Henry. If you can't show the land belongs to you legally, you're going to lose it."

"A lot of folks ain't got deeds to their land. It's passed down from one generation to another. It's just how it's done," Henry says protesting.

"That might be true. But you're the only one around here with hundreds of thousands of acres up for grabs. I need to see every deed you have to this ranch."

Henry is once again forced into silence, pondering his fate. Sinclair seems frustrated.

"I hope you're not wasting my time, Henry."

"You're getting paid, aren't you," Henry replies back sharply.

Sinclair is clearly upset at this turn of events.

It is a late summer night, and cooler evenings are becoming more frequent as fall begins to set in. Daisy and George sit outside on the front porch to enjoy the cool breeze. Katie is in McGovern at Andy's office working late on the case.

"Don't know where Katie gets so much spunk. She certainly didn't get it from me," George says to Daisy.

"Are you really planning to testify?" Daisy asks worriedly. She knows that no amount of pleading is going to keep George from doing what he wants once his mind is made up.

"The truth, the whole truth, and nothing but—so help me, God."

This has an effect on Daisy as she is thinking far off about something. She hesitates, then...

"George."

"Mmmm?"

"There's something I must tell you. About Katie. And... Patrick," Daisy begins.

"What is it? Something wrong?"

"You know that I have never loved another man before or since you?" Daisy adds apprehensively.

"Before you and I were married, I was with someone. I'm so very sorry, George. I was pregnant with the twins when you married me. I'm so very sorry. It's something I wished I'd never have to tell you."

George is stunned and in shock. He asks with great pain in his voice, "What are you saying, Daisy?"

"I've been so ashamed. And I didn't want the children to know who their father was, because you were meant to be their father."

George is thinking now, and slowly says, "What? Who?"

Seeing Daisy's wild look, George says,
"No.... No... Not Henry!"

"Henry Champion is their father," Daisy says,
with her heart breaking in watching George's
pain.

George is now pacing back and forth. He wants
to scream. He cannot take this.

"Henry and I ended up drinking one night at
that New Years Eve party. You were angry that
Henry was paying me attention, so you left with
Dolly. That was when it happened. Shortly
before we were together for good and you asked
me to marry you. I've hated him for taking
advantage of me."

George's eyes are wide and disbelieving.

 "I don't remember it happening at the time, but
I knew the next morning. Henry probably
doesn't remember it, either. I wanted you to be
their father, George. Henry doesn't know. He
must never know. No one but you knows now."

"How could you have not said anything. All
these years, Daisy?"

"I'm so sorry, George. It really pains me to tell
you. I wanted to take this secret to my grave.
But as evil as Henry is, he just could not be

their father."

She takes a step toward him for comfort, but
George steps back, still in cold shock. He is
crying now, too. He holds up his hands toward
her to stop her from getting close to him and
then walks out of the house.

"Katie is your daughter, George. She will always
be your daughter," Daisy yells after him.

George walks away from the farmhouse with
pain in his eyes, tears matting his face. He
keeps moving and feeling more lost than he has
ever felt in his life. George's thoughts are torn
up. How can the children he has raised not be
his flesh and blood? How can Patrick and Katie
who he has loved and guided not be his very
own? Finally finding himself far from home,
George stops and falls hard on his knees,
burying them into the dirt, as he continues to
sob his heart out. The sunset streaks across his
face with orange and golden hues, as the day's
light comes to an end.

The next morning, Katie is in the barn brushing down a mare as Daniel enters.

"Hi, Katie. Daisy told me where to find you."

"What do you want, Champion?"

"May I have a moment of your time to discuss the trial, Counselor?"

"You don't have an appointment," Katie answers barely amused.

"Didn't think an old friend needed one." Daniel pauses and then, "I'd like to help the families get their land back."

"Why would you go against King Henry?" Katie asks him.

"It's time to set things straight around here."

Not a word between them for a few moments.

"It hasn't been easy growing up with someone like Henry. He's damn mean. Maybe my mother would have made him a better man. Losing her only made him more brutal."

Katie wants to trust what he is saying. She

wants to believe he is the same old Daniel and has not been corrupted by Henry in the many years she has been away.

"Katie... I'm on your side on this thing. People have suffered too much because of my father. Folks deserve to get what belongs to them."

"Why should I believe you, Daniel?"

Looking into Katie's eyes in earnest, "'Cause you've known me all of my life. You know who I am."

Katie finally relents, realizing for the first time that life must have been dreadful all these years growing up with someone like Henry for a father. And even more painful not having his mother to protect him.

"I can't imagine what it's been like for you, Daniel."

They look into each other's faces for a few moments in silence. They are becoming friends again. They come close and embrace and stand there in each other's arms for a while.

Roy's Feed Store in Forgotten is a hangout of sorts for a lot of the men in Forgotten. Ranchers and farmers get together there and catch up on things while doing their business. Today, George walks in and approaches the owner, Roy.

"Morning, George," Roy greets him.

"Hiya, Roy."

"How long we got till the trial?"

"Maybe a week or so. Let's hope we have something to celebrate by Christmas. Just a bag of feed today, Roy."

Roy gestures to one of his employees.

"Twenty-pound bag of the usual feed for George, Tommy."

George hangs out at the counter for a few minutes with Roy.

"Folks all over gettin' real excited about seeing old Henry in a pickle," Roy says to George.

"Folks are just doing what's right," George responds.

"I wanna talk to you."

George recognizes the voice instantly. He turns to see Henry standing there.

"Don't you ever get tired of being you, Henry? It must really be a pain to wake up and be you every day."

The men in the store stop their socializing and shift their attention to Henry and George.

"You've always been a yellowbelly, George."

"And you're the devil's best friend."

Tommy hoists the bag of feed onto his shoulder and moves around Henry to exit. He stands by the door waiting on George. He does not want to miss this altercation.

"Thanks, Roy. Put it on my account," George says to Roy while ignoring Henry.

Henry's not going to go away it seems.

"I always felt real sorry for poor Daisy."

As George goes to leave, that slows him down and he stops, his back remaining to Henry.

"She's never had much of a life with you. Never could fathom how a beautiful woman like Daisy could end up with a disgustin' nothing like you," Henry says hatefully.

George turns, gazes at Henry's mug expression.

"You ain't good enough to even think about her. Everyone in town knows your own wife couldn't stand you. Bless her soul," George says.

"Daisy was the only woman I ever really wanted. Course, I was the only real man she ever had," Henry says with callous smugness on his face.

Well, that surely does it. George approaches Henry, grabbing a bailing hook off the counter, and laying it across Henry's face. George is livid, but in control.

"Go ahead, George. Kill me in front of our friends here."

"You ain't got any friends, Henry. I don't want you to die. I'm going to enjoy watching you lose everything," George says with a grin on his face.

Roy and some of the others find a proud grin on their lips as George hangs the hook in Henry's shirt pocket and walks away.

George looks back at him and says, "By the way, Henry. Daisy always retches at the mention of your name."

Henry hates it! His lips quiver, and his jaw quakes. George turns to leave, and Tommy is there holding the bag for him. Tommy grins as he follows George out to the truck with the bag of feed.

Daisy is weeding in the garden as George pulls up the road leading to the farmhouse. They have not spoken since she revealed the twin's paternity.

George walks up slowly toward her. She looks up at him and there is a long moment of silence.

George begins, "I know what you did was for the best, Daisy. You're a good woman."

Daisy has never been happier to see her husband. She looks up at him with appreciation.

"The thought of our children having been raised

by Henry is... Well, I just can't imagine it," George continues.

Katie stands and moves toward him and puts her arms around him. He holds her tightly in his arms.

"Thank you for giving me your children, Daisy."

"Thank you for understanding, my love. I couldn't have survived Henry taking my babies away."

George takes her hands and kisses them.

"Our babies," George responds.

"We have to tell Katie," Daisy says.

"This will hurt her deeply," George answers in a distressed voice.

CHAPTER 16
Shenanigans

A nice crowd is gathered at Mike's Pub. The same pub Daniel Champion has played for the past twenty years. The locals sit around drinking and listening to Daniel and his country band on stage. After all these years, he has become more talented than ever. Katie walks in, catches Daniel's eye, and walks over to the bar and orders a soda. Sitting a few barstools away is Byron Tate, a fairly well-known country music star, who is in town visiting Daniel, his college buddy. Byron notices Katie and comes over to her.

"Katie?! Byron asks.

"Byron Tate?! Wow! When did you get into town?" Katie asks, beginning to sound more like one of the locals. "I've heard so many songs of yours on the radio."

"I've heard a lot about you, too. Just got in this afternoon. Daniel and I are working on a duet together for a single. Looks like we're gonna release it soon," Byron says excitedly.

"That's great! It should do well considering both of your talents. But you know, Daniel. I don't think he would leave Forgotten."

"Well, the traveling performer life isn't for everyone. Being on the road constantly is hard. He loves his music and I guess that's what matters the most, right?" Byron replies.

"You've done very well for yourself. Love your last album."

"Thanks, Katie."

Daniel's song ends and walks over to join them.

"You're more talented than ever, man. You should get out of this town and head to Nashville," Byron says to his friend of many years.

"Naaa... I like this place. At least I know people here like my music."

"People would like your music no matter where you are, Daniel," Katie says, touching him warmly on the arm.

Their eyes connect and they both feel the affection between them.

"I admire you, Daniel," Byron says. "You've always been your own man. Even in college, you always did your own thing."

"Probably not as much as I admire you, Byron. You've always had the courage and talent to pursue your dreams. I'm too simple of a man... Fame and fortune don't mean much. Besides, this town has a way of sucking you in and won't let you leave."

"I escaped!" Katie quips.

Smiling at her Daniel says, "That's what you think."

"Amen! I can't seem to get away from my hometown, either. I go back every chance I get," Byron says.

Katie, Daniel, and Byron raise their glasses, and all say, "To hometowns!"

Katie is headed to her best friend's house this day. She has always made it a point to see Beth when she is in town, and it has been at least six months since she has been by. Beth's home is located in a modest, middle-class part of Forgotten. She ended up marrying an electrician from San Antonio, and they now have a couple of kids. Beth took Patrick's death just about as hard as they all did, and it took her a while to find her way back. As Katie pulls up in her dad's truck, Beth's little girls are running around outside playing when Katie walks up to the house.

"Aunt Katie!" Two little girls run up and hug Katie.

"Hi, sweeties! I've missed you, girls," Katie says to them picking them up one at a time and giving them a kiss on their cheeks.

Beth opens the front door and goes out to greet Katie. They hug hello and then walk inside.

Beth quickly gets to the point. "I heard you saw Daniel."

"How on earth would you know that so quickly?" Katie asks with a funny look.

My neighbor's brother saw you at Mike's Pub last night. He said you two looked real cozy and friendly, laughing and---"

"Beth! We most certainly were not cozy," Katie replies, stretching out the word 'cozy.' But yes, I've seen him a few times. We're trying to put the past behind us. Well, at least I am."

"How's that going?" Beth asks.

"I've forgiven him about my brother. I know it wasn't something he would have wanted to happen to his best friend."

"And?" Beth wants to know more.

"I don't know. He will always be my first love."

"And maybe your last?" Beth says to her.

Katie does not respond as they look at one another and then laugh.

"I don't think so, Beth. Soon enough I'll be back in Los Angeles. Back to my life."

The next day, George is driving down the highway headed into town to do some business. Soon, George's eyes react when he sees Henry's Suburban approaching in the opposite direction. Henry gets excited to see George's old truck coming toward him. He lets out a laugh and turns up the music on the radio.

"This is going to be fun!" Henry laughs out loud.

Henry suddenly pulls into George's lane. It seems he is up to his old tricks and playing 'chicken' with George again. The vehicles are headed for each other, but the determined look on George's face says he is not going to be the 'chicken' this time. This is it!

Henry's chuckling to himself, obviously thinking George will pull off at the last minute as he has always done in the past. But he is wrong this time! Realizing he is about to collide with George head-on, he swerves at the last possible second, but it is too late. The loud sound of the crash and screeching of brakes is heard far and wide. The vehicles sideswipe each other and are forced to spin down the highway. The old Chevy skids and goes into a ditch. Henry's Suburban slides into a bank on the other side.

Nearby, Daniel is driving a Champion Ranch truck through a field. He hears the accident and accelerates, leaving a rooster tail of dust behind him.

Henry is trying to move in his vehicle, but he cannot. His leg is severely hurt and bleeding. Otherwise, everything else seems okay. Back in George's Chevy, George is not moving.

Daniel's truck pulls up next to the Suburban and sees his dad.

"What the hell happened, Dad?" Daniel yells.

"That crazy Baker sumbitch tried to kill me!"

"What?" Sarcastically, Daniel adds, "Sure he did. Are you okay?"

"It's my leg."

Daniel helps his father out of the Suburban, sitting him in his truck.   He then runs over to George in the Chevy. As Daniel opens the door, he sees that George is still breathing. Daniel lifts him out of the truck and carries him to his pickup, laying him down into the flatbed. George opens his eyes to see his old Chevy totaled in the ditch.

"Are you okay, George?"

"My truck... my truck!" is all that George can say.

"At least you're going to be okay, George."

George's face is scrunched up with the look of a wild animal who has been hurt and captured. He is thinking that the pain of losing his truck is worse than the pain he is feeling from his cut up arm right now.

"You're alive, George. Forget the truck. Your arm is bleeding," Daniel says to him.

"Daniel!" Henry calls out to his son.

"Can you get me home?" George asks of Daniel.

"You need to go to the hospital, George."

"I wanna go home," George sounds serious.

"Alright, I'll call Doc out to your place when I get you home," Daniel replies.

"Are you going to help me or what?" Henry is still yelling for his son from inside of the cab of Daniel's truck.

Daniel hops into the truck and drives away headed for George's farm. As they arrive at the farmhouse, Daisy sees them pull up and becomes frantic.

"Oh my gosh, what happened?!" Daisy yells.

Daniel rushes to get George out of the flatbed.

"Daisy, would you please call Doc and tell him

I've asked him to please come out here to see George right away?"

Daisy runs into the house to call the doctor.

Helping George into the house, Daniel asks, "Where's Katie, George?"

"I dropped her off at the Cut and Curl in town."

"I'll pick her up," Daniel says as he helps George onto the sofa.

"What happened, Daniel?" Daisy asks more calmly now.

"My father was probably up to his old shenanigans again."

"Henry has to be stopped. He's becoming more unhinged by the day and his hatred for George is out of control."

Henry is still yelling for Daniel from outside.

"Dangit, boy! I'm bleeding to death out here."

"Go help him, I'll be okay," George says to him.

"He's fine. I'm so sorry. I'm so ashamed about all of this."

"It isn't your fault, Daniel. You know... Daisy has always been fond of you."

Daisy adds, "I know you're a good man, Daniel."

"Daisy forgave you immediately. I've tried but it's been hard. Daisy has always said you didn't acquire the Champion thirst for blood."

Daisy nods in agreement at Daniel.

CHAPTER 17
The Date

Sinclair is back in town for the trial. She has accepted Henry's invitation to dine in Forgotten's nicest restaurant, Lucky D's BBQ. There are many cars parked outside this evening, which is usually a good sign the food is delicious.

Henry has not been out on a date with a lady in years. His palms are sweaty as he clutches the steering wheel. He is thinking his breathing is a little fast from nerves, as he tells himself to relax. Sinclair, on the other hand, is sitting pretty in the passenger's side of his Suburban. He glances at her frequently. She is wearing a baby blue colored suit, and he likes the way her light blue eyes match it so well. He wonders to himself if she is feeling as anxious about this date, too? Sinclair is cool and calm and does not display a bit of anxiety. Although Henry sees it as a date, Sinclair is merely out for a business dinner and nothing more. The two could not be further apart on their intentions.

Lucy, the waitress, greets them at the door of the establishment. Since the accident, Henry is now sporting a crutch and hobbles into the place. Although he tries his best to pull her chair out and be a gentleman for her, it is too much with the crutch under his arm, and almost stumbles into Sinclair.

"It's okay, Henry. I've got this."

Henry is trying his best to be the perfect date. As they get comfortable, Lucy brings them a couple of menus.

"Thanks for accompanying me to dinner tonight, Sinclair."

"You're welcome, Henry."

"It's been a very long time since I dined in the company of a lady... especially one as lovely and classy as you."

"Thank you, Henry. And thank you for the invitation to dinner."

Henry's thinking this last comment from Sinclair may be a positive sign that she is enjoying his company, and happy to be out to dinner with him. After all, Henry does not consider Sinclair to be the type of woman to be out with a man in which she is not interested.

Lucy walks up to them now to take their orders. There are many ranchers and farmers out with their families having dinner. It seems Sinclair and Henry are getting a lot of attention tonight.

Somehow, Sinclair seems out of place in this environment. Her expensive clothing, shoes, and purse do not seem to fit in with all the locals in their comfy blue jeans. She sticks out like a sore thumb. She notices all the staring, but Sinclair has never really worried much for what people think about her.

"You want your usual pork ribs, Henry? I'll get you a bib," Lucy says to Henry, loudly accentuating the word bib, and getting even more attention from the other customers. She obviously knows him well as a regular.

Henry is now turning red with embarrassment and notices all eyes on him.

"That sounds like *fun*! We can eat with our *fingers!*" Sinclair says, happily teasing him.

"No, I don't want the damn... mmm. Pardon me, the darn ribs, Lucy," George says with awkwardness written all over his face.

Lucy is looking at Sinclair now. "I'll have the baked chicken and pinto beans, please."

"Please bring me the ribeye, Lucy. You know how I like it," Henry says, trying to sound more gracious.

Sinclair is enjoying watching this insecure and embarrassed side of Henry.

"Let me see your wine selection, would you, Lucy?" Henry adds.

"What wine selection might that be, Henry?" Lucy asks, mocking him a bit.

Henry is feeling completely uncomfortable now and says, "Never mind. Just brings us a couple of whatever wine you got, alright?"

"I'll see what I can find," Lucy says and runs off.

Henry is now beet red with embarrassment.

Taking some pity on him, Sinclair says, "Has anyone told you how cute you are when you blush?"

Now, Henry's sinking into his chair, wishing he could disappear. Not many people have seen Henry this vulnerable.

"Here I am, trying to make a good impression on a fine lady such as yourself, and I look like a damn fool."

"No, you don't. You're sweet. You can be very charming when you want to be, Henry."

"No one has ever called me cute or sweet."

"You should practice being nicer. You have quite the reputation, you know?" Sinclair proclaims, making Henry's eyes open wider with curiosity.

Henry decides it is probably best not to include any negative topic in their conversation tonight and changes his mind about asking her what types of things she has heard about him.

They regard each other for a moment, then Henry asks, "Why aren't you married, anyway?"

"Direct, aren't you, Henry? My husband passed away six years ago. I haven't found anyone who is even half as wonderful enough to replace him."

"Maybe if the right man came along," Henry persists.

"If, and maybe!" Sinclair answers half-heartedly.

Henry is smitten with Sinclair and enjoys looking at her. He is fond of the way the dimples on her cheeks pop in and out when she smiles. He is thinking he is extremely interested in Sinclair. Wow, she really is something special, but he is certain a woman like Sinclair would never give a man like him the time of day.

Lucy walks up now with a couple of wine coolers and says, "Are you gonna be needin' some fancy glasses for these, or you gonna drink it straight out of the bottle?"

Henry and Sinclair look at one another, and then start laughing out loud. It is so weird to see Henry laughing. Sinclair thinks to herself how great it is to see him like this. Henry's laughter feels genuine and strange all at the same time. Even with the embarrassing moments, Henry is having the best time he has had in years.

CHAPTER 18
The Trial

George Baker sits on his front porch reading the Forgotten newspaper. On the front page is a headline which says, 'Champion Land Deed Trial to Begin Tomorrow.'

George reads for a while, then sets the paper down, and pauses for a moment. He travels back into his memories, remembering that brutal day when Henry's grandfather, John Champion, came calling on his family. Long ago flashes of moments fill his mind's eye. The same heartbreaking tears that fell from his eyes as a boy hiding in the brush, those same tears once again flow freely down his face, as he recalls the murders of his family. He hears the cries of his mother and sisters as they tried to flee, the horrifying sounds etched on his mind forever. He can still see his father fall lifeless to the ground, as Henry's grandfather shoots his Pa in the back as he tries to run.

"It's high time your family's name pays for the crimes you and your kin have committed, Henry," George mutters to himself.

George stands and walks over to a nearby old oak tree. His hands struggle a bit with a large stone on the ground. He removes the stone and digs around a bit. He removes an old cloth bag with something in it. He pulls out the old box he retrieved from the fire in his childhood home all those many years ago.

Just like the name of his town, Forgotten, so many crimes and bad deeds had long been forgotten. Generations had come and gone, and the time had come for many to remember. All the dirty deeds and sins of past generations, long lost and mostly buried, were coming to life once again. George wanted for everyone to recall what happened in this town all those years ago, the tragic events that had haunted this town like ghosts for decades. Many families had suffered unimaginable horrors just as he had. So many ghosts that had wandered about lost and forgotten were about to be heard from again.

George's eyes are full of tears and reflection. There is a cautious gleam in them as he closes them in prayer. He prays there is justice in store for him and for everyone else who has lost their heritage. George will fight for his family's legacy.

The day of the trial has finally arrived. The Forgotten courthouse is full of citizens from town. The wooden floors have been polished nicely, in preparation for the big event. It is a small-town courthouse, and the court room's size reflects this, so it is very crowded. There has never been a trial like this one in Forgotten. Everyone seems anxious, awaiting the trial to begin. There is not an empty seat in the room, while many others stand in the back, and those who could not get into the courtroom are now standing outside. All the expected troupe is present including Andy Cruz, Katie, Sinclair Davis, Henry Champion, Sheriff Pete, Daisy, Mr. Lozano, and all the rest. George Baker is nowhere in sight.

Everyone stands as the Bailiff requests, and Judge Raye comes in and takes his official place. The twelve-person Jury is present, and you wonder how many of them are really going to toss Henry the proverbial bone knowing of his wide-spread reputation. How many of these jurors has Henry paid off? Mr. Lozano is called to the witness stand. After the swearing in, Katie rises to question him.

Holding up a deed for the jurors to see, Katie asks, "Mr. Lozano, would you please tell the court exactly how you acquired this document?"

"My Papa died a couple of years ago. We left his old house alone for a while. My wife and I had to get it cleaned up and emptied sometime back. We found the deed in the old family bible."

Sinclair yells, "Objection. Mr. Lozano is making an assumption of legal ownership, Your Honor! It hasn't been proven."

"Sustained," Judge Raye says to the court.

"No further questions," Katie says to the Judge.

"Ms. Davis?" the Judge says to Sinclair.

"No questions, Your Honor."

"The witness may be dismissed," Judge Raye says.

"Thank you, Mr. Lozano," Katie says as Mr. Lozano leaves the stand.

Henry sits there brooding as he glances around. Andy Cruz rises and calls Mrs. Talley to the stand. She is a cute, elderly lady, and quite a character. She walks up slowly to the front of the courtroom, and Andy helps her get comfortable and seated on the witness stand. Mrs. Talley offers everyone a big smile and seems more than excited and ready for her

questioning. She is sworn in and Andy is ready
to go.

"Hello, Mrs. Talley," Andy says kindly to her.

Mrs. Talley smiles sweetly as a response.

"If we may ask a lady's age – how old are you,
Mrs. Talley?"

"I'm 89, young man. Be 90 in December."

"Mrs. Talley, please tell the court what you saw
that summer night. The night you lost your
land and home."

"I's eight an' a half. My Pa was gettin' the field
ready for plantin'. Pa worked to the bone takin'
care of my Ma and us six girls. Ma and 'im tried
havin' a boy to hep'im in the fields, but each
time got 'em a girl. Guess my Pa had no male
bullets in 'im."

A few chuckles and laughs from the courtroom,
even the Judge smiles a little.

"What happened, Mrs. Talley," Andy asks her
again.

"Well, my Pa never believed the outdoors was
for womenfolk. Shit—we had to wear bonnets to

protect us from the harsh Texas sun," Mrs. Talley says.

A few more chuckles and giggles from the locals in the courtroom.

"Mrs. Talley, please try to refrain from cursing in my courtroom," Judge says in an admonishing but kindly tone.

She continues, "Okay. Those days were hotter 'n a goat's ass in heat."

Everyone in the courtroom laughs out loud, everyone of course, except Henry and Sinclair.

"Awww, Maybelle." Judge Raye says trying hard not to smile. Mrs. Talley is so cute and innocent sitting there that no one expects that sort of language to come out of her mouth.

Sinclair rises and says, "Relevancy here, Your Honor. Can we get to the point? The witness is narrating."

Andy interjects, "Ancestral history, Your Honor. The testimony will conjoin."

Sinclair is clearly getting frustrated. She stands and says, "May we approach the bench?"

Judge Raye motions Andy, Katie, and Sinclair forward as Mrs. Talley sits in the witness stand as sweet as she can be.

The Judge is beginning to get frustrated with Andy. "Are we going to get actual testimony, counselor?"

"I can't see how this nonsense is relevant," Sinclair fumes.

"This is an elderly witness, Your Honor," Katie pleads.

"If we want to get testimony sometime this century, we must allow her to narrate," adds Andy.

"I'll agree, but direct your witness, Mr. Cruz."

Andy nods at him, and Sinclair and Katie return to their seats.

"Mrs. Talley, could you tell us how your family came to lose your land?" Andy asks her gently.

Becoming more serious, Mrs. Talley removes her straw bonnet with tiny yellow flowers on the brim and begins to share her story.

"Late one night, during a bright full moon, some bad men came ridin'. My sisters and I woke up and our room was on fire. Our Ma come in and took us outside. I seen several men on horseback with torches. One of the men shot our Pa. Then they rode away.

"Did you recognize any of the men that night, Mrs. Talley?"

"Sure as hell!" Looking at Henry, she says, "John Champion and his gang killed my Pa! John was a young man then, but he was no good all of his miserable life."

Henry Champion rises. He's furious and says, "She's lying! My grandfather did no such thing."

"Sit down, Mr. Champion," Judge Raye orders.

Sinclair forces Henry back into his seat.

Mrs. Talley continues, "John Champion killed my Pa and took the land... and kep' killin' and stealin' his whole damn life."

"Your Honor!" Sinclair says to no avail.

The courtroom is buzzing with whispers and talking. Henry is clearly the most upset and uncomfortable we have ever seen.

Judge Raye bangs his gavel, "Order in this

courtroom now!"

"Your Honor, I fail to see, once again, the
relevancy, and how it pertains to this case.
John Champion is not on trial," Sinclair states.

"If Your Honor and counsel will permit me to
proceed with the questioning, the testimony will
establish the importance and pertinency," Andy
says with confidence.

"Proceed then, Mr. Cruz."

"One more question, Mrs. Talley. Who is in
possession of your land today?"

Pointing directly at Henry with a trembling
hand, "Henry Champion."

The courtroom buzzes again.

"No more questions."

Andy sits as Sinclair stands.

"Mrs. Talley, why didn't you come forward with
this story before now?" Sinclair asks her with
an edge in her tone.

Sinclair is standing closer to Mrs. Talley now.

"You gets old, and after a while, not much to be

'fraid of no more, 'cept dyin. Couldn't do that without settin' things straight for my Pa."

Sinclair responds, "No more questions."

Sinclair walks over and sits next to Henry. He is fuming.

"Why didn't you drill her or something? I thought you were on my side of this mess," Henry asks her angrily.

"I am on your side, Henry. But we're not going to get very far by badgering an elderly lady."

"You're dismissed, Maybelle," Judge says to Mrs. Talley.

"This court will resume at nine o'clock tomorrow morning," Judge says as he bangs the gavel.

"All rise," the Bailiff says.

Everyone exits the Courtroom. People pour out into the street and head in all different directions.

Katie and Daisy notice George pulling up to the Courthouse in a brand-new truck. He gets out as they walk over to him.

Katie lets out a whistle as she checks out the truck and then gives him a hug.

Daisy hugs him and says, "We missed you today. But I'm glad you listened to me and didn't come."

"I wasn't up for it. Never in the mood to see Henry," George says.

"Best you just stay away for now, dear."

"I like your new truck, Dad. It's about time," Katie says cheerfully as she checks out the truck.

George's brand new, blue 1976 Ford F150 is a beauty. Katie walks around it now admiring it, and then hops into the truck to check out the interior.

"Overpriced hunk of metal, that's all. Can you believe it? Four thousand dollars! I got robbed. Don't make 'em like they used to, that's for sure," George grumbles.

Henry, Daniel, and Sinclair walk out of the courthouse. Henry sees George, and of course, cannot resist giving him a hard time. Henry is using a cane now, and George still has his arm in a sling.

"Get the hell out of my way, Baker!" Henry says purposely going out of his way to cross him.

"You're truly a disappointment, Henry. All these years, I thought you were smarter than you've turned out to be," George says in a taunting voice with pleasure on his face.

Henry lashes back, "You're a crazy old poke!"

"And you're pathetic, standing there leaning on an old man's stick. Can't say I'm sorry to see you this way," George says stinging Henry a little more.

"You're a damn loser, George. You will never get my land."

The animosity between the men is intense. They are standing with their faces within inches of each other. At the moment, they look like a couple of wild animals ready to attack, spitting and teeth gnashing as they talk.

Daisy can just imagine George and Henry hitting the ground and fighting like twelve-year olds, just like they did when they were kids. Katie and Daniel can also picture their fathers coming to blows.

Daisy is tired of it and says, "You got three good legs and three good arms between you. You both have messed up hearts. When is this going to stop?"

She grabs George by the arm and says, "Let's go get something to eat, dear. C'mon, Katie."

Daniel pulls his father away, "Let's go, Dad." Sinclair and Daniel drag Henry away from the scene.

Katie and Daniel look back at one other with concern as they all walk away.

CHAPTER 19
All on the Table

George and Daisy are sitting at the kitchen table as Katie walks in the door.

She notices their glum faces and says to them, "What's wrong with you two? You look like someone died."

"We need to talk to you, Katie," Daisy says quietly.

Daisy has never been more afraid to talk to Katie. Her hands shake as she forces a small smile for her daughter. She worries Katie may never forgive her for this.

"Please sit down, sweetie," George says.

"Okay, you guys are freaking me out," Katie remains standing, her face now clouded with concern.

"There are things I've been wanting to tell you, Katie. I've waited because I don't want to hurt you," Daisy begins.

At Daisy's hesitation, "I know you would never intentionally hurt me, Mom."

"First of all, you know Daniel is adopted."

"Yes, Mom. The whole town knows that. What does that have to do with me?"

"There's more to know, Katie," her dad adds.

"It's going to hurt you, but I hope you will come to understand that it was the best I could do for you. So... I want you to know it all," Daisy says with tears already in her eyes.

Katie's worried expression hurts Daisy, as her daughter sits at the table to hear the secret her mother has carried within her all these many years.

"I hope you will forgive me for what I'm about to tell you, Katie."

"Mom, you're really scaring me."

"I wanted to keep this my secret alone. But I couldn't any longer. With all that's happening, it's important that you know the truth."

"Please, Mom. I want to know."

After Daisy is done telling her the story of Henry, Katie lowers her head on her arms on the table and begins to cry. Her parents try to console her, but Katie is devastated as her body trembles with tears, pain, anger, and confusion. Katie stands and goes to hug her father. He rises from the table and holds her in his arms as she weeps.

"I can't believe all of this. I want you to be my Father."

"I am your dad, Katie. I will always be your only dad."

"I will never accept Henry as my father. Never."

George and Daisy do their best to comfort her. They know that with a little time, Katie will come to understand.

Daisy stands and they all hold each other. The women cry as George watches them in sadness.

The trial has been going on all week, with different families trying to stake their claim to their lands by testifying. Dozens more families have now come forward and the case has exploded into several towns with more lawsuits being filed.

Today, Felder has been on the stand speaking his truth. Henry is sitting in the courtroom looking bored and appears as if he is about to fall asleep.

"No more questions, Mr. Felder," Katie says, now at the stand wrapping up the questioning.

As Felder steps down and walks to his seat, George Baker walks into the courtroom. As always, the room is full of the locals who seem to be enjoying the proceedings. Daisy sees George and shoots him a worried look. George looks at her nervously but is determined to be here.

Katie rises from her chair and says, "I call George Baker to the stand."

Henry's eyes open wide and he straightens up in his chair as he watches George walk up to the witness stand. There is a lot of excitement in the courtroom at the mention of George's name. Daisy shoots a warm smile to George, as she knows him too well. George always knew he was going to do this regardless of what anyone said. He had to set things straight for his parents and siblings, no matter the cost. George is feeling confident now, motivated by a sudden sense of freedom from the past.

"Could you state your name for the court, please," Katie says to her Dad.

"You know my name, Katie."

"For the court, please. State your name."

George feels silly since every person in the room most likely knows who he is.

"George Baker."

"Mr. Baker, I'd like to begin with your family. How did they die?" Katie asks him calmly.

Henry is now wearing a look of horror on his face. He is thinking back to that long-ago day when he accompanied his grandfather to George's family farm. The truth continues to be exposed before the court, and Henry knows that life will never be the same again for him. He is now fully aware the Champion name is about to pay for the crimes of the past. The past, it seems, has finally caught up to Henry.

With confidence, George begins. "It was a few hours past sunrise in the Spring of 1928. I was almost twelve then. Got a new shotgun for Christmas. I was out in the brush hunting jack rabbits for supper."

George tells the courtroom of the horrors he experienced that day. Hearing his Mother's scream in the distance. Hiding in the brush while watching his entire family murdered by John Champion and his men. Witnessing his sisters drown and brother and father shot in the back as they tried to run away.

George is now pointing at Henry. "You were there, Henry. You saw John Champion, your grandfather, shoot my Pa in the back!"

"You're a damn liar, George."

The courtroom is going crazy now. Everyone is talking and even the jurors seemed shocked to hear this.

Sinclair stands and says, "This is ridiculous, Your Honor. John Champion is not on trial here."

"I will allow the questioning, Counselor." Looking at George, he adds, "Do not talk to anyone in the courtroom. Answer the attorney's questions only, Mr. Baker. If anyone else speaks out, I'll instruct the Bailiff to throw them out and hold them in contempt. You may proceed, Ms. Baker."

"And following your tragedy, Mr. Baker. What did you do?" Katie asks.

"I went to live with my Uncle Wally by the farmhouse I've lived in ever since. The Champions took our land. When John Champion died, Henry never once tried to set things straight with me... or with anyone else. He knew. He's always known. And he did nothing about it."

Katie asks, "Where's the deed to your family's land now, the property by the river?"

George reaches into his coat pocket and pulls out the deed he rescued so long ago. He slams it down before the Judge and looks at Henry and sends him a smirk of his own.

"The deed has been registered and validated, Your Honor," George adds with satisfaction.

To calm things down the judge says, "Let's take an hour recess."

Moments later, people come out of the courtroom to take a break. Henry sits alone in the courtroom pondering his fate. Sinclair walks back in and sits next to him. Sinclair has a look of pity for him as she thinks to herself there really is not much more she can do.

Sinclair wonders now if Henry has paid off the judge or jurors, since she knows he has spent his life buying his way out of everything.

Henry looks frightened... as if he is about to lose it all. He seems more fragile now, and appears small, as if he has lost his stature.

Feeling sorry for him, Sinclair says, "Are you alright, Henry? Can I get you some water?"

"I'm fine."

It is clear that Henry is anything but okay at this moment. She takes her hand and places it on Henry's.

"No matter what happens today, Henry. I'm here. I really do care about what happens to you."

"Why should I matter to you? I'm just a sorry SOB."

"Well, I've seen a side of Henry that not many people get to see. You're not all bad," Sinclair says, trying her best to cheer him up.

Henry takes a good look at Sinclair. She has been decent and kind to him. He has grown very fond of her.

People are beginning to come back in. Daisy and George walk past Henry and sit down in the front row. George seems happy, relaxed, and confident as he waits on the trial to resume. Sometime later, an expert in land deed authentication is sitting on the witness stand.

The deed expert is now saying, "These documents have been recorded and are in registration with the Texas Land Office of Bandera County, with the exception of evidence marked 33. It will be recorded and registered within a few days."

Days later, the courtroom is crowded again as all await the verdict. Everyone seems apprehensive but excited as the judge comes into the courtroom to face them. Judge Raye has always sided with Henry in the past. Sandy Gutierrez wonders if Henry has paid him off as she believes he has done before. Would the jury be fair? People are uneasy as they wait for the judge to render the decision. Katie and Andy are concerned now, as the Judge's expression seems indifferent. They can definitely see this thing going one way or the other.

Judge Raye is now reading the verdict. People hold their breath in anticipation. As the verdict is read, the courtroom explodes in excitement!

The people have won their case against Henry!
Everyone in the courtroom is jubilant, except
for Henry Champion. Sinclair looks concerned.

Henry stands and says to the judge, "I'll make
you pay for this!"

Judge Raye looks at Henry, shakes his head, and
sneers. Not even the judge will be bullied and
intimidated by Henry any longer.

Henry looks devastated as Daniel and Sinclair
lead him out of the courtroom.

Moments later, people are pouring out of the
courthouse. The families congratulate one
another as they happily celebrate their victory.

"Thanks, Andy, Katie. You guys pulled it off,"
George says to them as they are standing on the
sidewalk.

"We're so proud of you both!" Daisy adds.

Looking at Katie, Andy says, "Couldn't have
done it without you."

Sheriff Pete is there congratulating Katie and
Andy, as well.

"Thanks, Pete!" Katie says while planting a kiss

on his cheek.

"Hey, don't I rate one of those," Andy says teasing Katie.

Katie gives Andy a kiss on the cheek and hugs him. They are congratulated by more of the families as they come over to say thank you.

"It was hard work but actually fun... and worth it!" Andy says to Katie. "How about escorting an old friend to the celebration over at Mike's Pub tonight. There's a lot to celebrate before you go back to Los Angeles."

"Sounds like a great time, Andy!"

"Great. See you later. Bye, Sheriff. See you all later. George, Daisy."

Everyone says their goodbyes to Andy as he walks away.

"Well, I'm back on duty, folks," Sheriff Pete says.

"See you, Sheriff!" More goodbyes from the folks.

Daniel, Henry, and Sinclair exit the courthouse. Henry's eyes find George's. George dons his Stetson and tips his hat to Henry, just as Henry has done to him in the past. Henry looks shattered. Daniel and Katie exchange a warm glance as he and Sinclair lead Henry away. Daniel helps his father into the truck, as his leg is still giving him problems. Sinclair stands on the curb. Henry rolls down his window to say goodbye to her. He simply gazes at her and cannot find any words to say. Henry reaches for her hand, and she places hers over his.

She says sadly, "I'm so sorry, Henry. I wish I could have done more."

Henry takes his other hand and places it over hers and says, "You're one of the innocents, Sinclair. You're a good woman."

"Please take care of yourself, Henry. Goodbye."

Daniel drives away from the curb and heads on down the street. Henry sees Sinclair through the passenger's side rearview mirror getting smaller, but no less significant as she stands by the road with her hand in the air waving goodbye. Before long, she disappears from view. Henry realizes he will probably die without ever having the love of a woman.

Daniel and Henry drive the entire way back to the Champion Ranch without saying a word. It is painfully clear to Daniel that there is nothing he can say to his father right now. There are no words to console him. The only things Henry has left are a few thousand acres surrounding the Estate. The rest of the land is gone. A lot of cattle must be sold to pay the legal fees. In their generosity, the families were kind enough to let Henry stay in his home. The only home he has ever known. The few thousand acres would still allow him to make a living.

CHAPTER 20
Celebration

The celebration at Mike's Pub is well underway when Katie, George, and Daisy stroll in. Daniel is looking particularly handsome tonight, wearing a black Stetson, white shirt, nicely starched blue jeans, and black cowboy boots. Katie cannot help admiring him and checking him out. Daniel's heart skips a beat as their eyes meet from across the room.

Daniel thinks to himself, "This girl still shakes my world," finding himself with sweaty palms and a nervous smile. He smiles as he recalls the many times they played together as kids, the great times they had together in high school, and he cannot believe she is back in his life again after so many painful years.

The song ends and the crowd cheers as people stop dancing. The Mayor of Forgotten goes up on the stage and takes the mic.

"Let's all give another round of applause for Forgotten's very own country music talent, Daniel Champion and his wonderful band.

The crowd goes crazy cheering for their homegrown band.

"And now," the Mayor continues, "We have a special surprise for you folks today!"

The crowd goes quiet in anticipation, as the Mayor says, "All the way from Nashville, coming here to help us celebrate tonight, and a good friend of Daniel's, please give a big Forgotten welcome to country music star, Byron Tate!"

The patrons go nuts, cheering, whistling, and clapping. Byron Tate walks onto the stage where he is greeted with a big hug from Daniel. The Mayor hands the mic to Byron.

"Hello, everybody!" The crowd cheers again!

"How would ya'll like your local country star and my old friend, Daniel, to join me up here?"

The crowd cheers as Daniel joins Byron at the mic.

"Daniel and I are gonna sing a song we wrote that's gonna be released real soon. You can all say you heard it live here first!"

There is more encouraging clapping and cheering from the crowd.

Byron Nelson continues, "The song is called, '*I Will Always Remember*.' Danny and I collaborated, I wrote the music, and he wrote the lyrics."

Daniel takes the mic and looking straight at Katie he says, "The lyrics in the song are about finding that one true love and then losing her. But hopefully, not forever."

Katie finds herself wondering if the song Daniel wrote is for her. Her face is warm and flushed. Daniel continues to gaze her way as they start singing. Katie, George, and Daisy look on impressed as Daniel and Byron sing their duet. The harmonizing is beautiful, and everyone is moved by the song.

"Wow, they are really great," George says.

"Daniel is so talented," Katie adds.

"Katie, please stay. Don't go back to Los Angeles," George says pleading.

"I want you to both come back to L.A. with me. I can take care of you there," Katie says in earnest.

Shocked at her request, George says, "We're country folk, Katie. We belong here. The big city would swallow us up whole."

Katie knows her parents would be miserable in Los Angeles. Although there is so much to love about the Southern California lifestyle, she does struggle there sometimes. She can imagine how much harder it would be for them. She would have to make more time to come and see them. She would have to ask for a lighter workload at the law firm in order to get away from work more.

"I really do understand why you didn't want me to know about Henry, Mom," Katie says to Daisy.

Daisy looks at Katie with love and says, "You don't know how much that means to me, dear."

"Dad, I can't imagine not having you in my life... as my dad... and having someone like Henry to deal with all my life."

"I've been praying you would understand, Katie," Daisy says to her.

"And I can't imagine not having either of you pestering me and driving me nuts," George says to lighten the tone.

"Well, if you're not coming with me to L.A., we're going to hire you some help, Dad. There's no good reason for you to do the farming all by yourself. Besides, you want me to sleep at night and not worry so much about you killing yourself every day, right?"

"Oh, alright. I knew the day would come when I needed to take it easier." George says giving in.

Katie and Daisy are happy to hear him finally admit this.

But George quickly adds, "Not saying I'm retiring, though."

Daisy and Katie look at him and smile. They both know George will work until his last breath. It is all he has ever known, and they understand it makes him happy.

Byron is starting to sing another song, as Daniel walks off the stage and heads toward Katie.

"Here comes, Daniel," Daisy says as she winks at Katie.

Katie grins and gives her Mom the look of 'Don't embarrass me, Mother.'

"Hi, George!" Daniel says, as he tips his hat to Daisy. "Hi, Daisy!"

George and Daisy greet him, and Daisy says, "You're so talented, Daniel. I think we'll be losing you to Nashville any day now, huh?"

"I'm not going anywhere, ma'am. I would get lost in the big city."

"That's what I've been trying to tell Katie, too! You're talented, but don't let anyone tell you that you belong somewhere you don't!" George says to Daniel while patting him on the back.

"Thank you," Daniel says to George. "At least someone understands."

Daisy and George dance away to the dancefloor. At the moment, Andy Cruz walks up to Katie and Daniel.

"I've been looking all over for you, Katie. Moving in on my date, Champion?" Andy says to Daniel.

"Listen, Andy. Could I have a word with Katie for a moment?"

"Sure," Andy replies. "I'll get us a couple of drinks, Katie."

As Andy walks away, Daniel sits next to Katie.

"How's Henry?" Katie asks.

"Not good. He's been drinking a lot more than usual... and that's really bad... He has serious heart problems."

"Those two stubborn men have given each other heart trouble, fighting their entire lives." Noticing his changed expression, Katie adds, "What is it, Daniel?"

"I'd like it if you would stay this time. We could settle down, have some kids. It's not too late. Marry me, Katie. I love you. I've never stopped loving you."

Katie is completely caught by surprise and does not know what to say to him.

He waits patiently. She finally answers and says, "My life is in L.A. My work is there. I'm not a farmer's daughter anymore. I don't know that I can live here, Daniel."

Daniel is feeling heartbroken, abandoned, and humiliated all at the same time.

"Still running away..." There is a long pause, and he is not going to beg, "Hope you find what you're looking for, Katie."

"You, too, Daniel. You deserve to be happy."

Daniel stands, gazes into her eyes for a few moments, then tips her hat to her and walks away.

Katie painfully watches him go back into the crowd and disappear.

"Here you are," Andy says as he walks up to the table with the drinks.

"Everything okay, Katie?" Andy says as he notices the somber look on her face.

Katie does not respond to his question. She faces him and gives him a half-forced smile.

The Forgotten Jail is a busy place this same evening. Officer Ortega is shoving Willy Watson and Johnny Spader, both now handcuffed, into the jail. He walks them down a long hall, removes their handcuffs and puts them in a jail cell.

Sheriff Pete saunters up to the cell and says to them, "Welcome home, boys. We've been waiting for you two a long time. Finally got caught in the act red-handed. Thank you for finally being less careful. I hope you'll make yourselves comfortable."

Back at the Champion Estate, Henry is in another drunken stupor tonight. He is alone in his library wallowing in his misery.

While the town is celebrating his demise, he takes another bottle out of the cabinet and opens it. He gets a glass and pours himself another drink. He walks over and stands in front of the painting of his grandfather, John Champion.

In a sudden rage, Henry flings the almost full glass of whiskey at the painting. It falls and shatter into pieces on the white stone hearth below. Henry is a broken man. He falls into a chair and sobs like a child.

CHAPTER 21
Los Angeles

Katie is back home in L.A. It is now November of 1976, and even though it has only been several months since she left, it seems like forever since she was here. The city seems different, almost foreign, but it feels nice to be back in the big city. A car honks and then cuts her off on the freeway.

"Welcome home," she laughs.

It was incredibly difficult to leave her parents this time. It has always been hard to say goodbye before, but this time was much more distinct and painful. She now finds herself worrying more about her dad, and what would happen to her mom if he got sick again, or worse, if they lost him. She had made sure before she left Forgotten that George had a farmhand to help him with the work. Katie pulls up her street and parks in front of her home, gets her suitcase out of the trunk, and walks to the front door. As she ambles in with her bags, she smells the musty odor of an aged house that has not had any fresh air in it for a lengthy period of time.

Katie looks around her homey, little cottage. It is a pretty, cozy place, and it has been home for the past ten years. Now, for the first time, she feels rather foreign in her own home. She notices the uneven paint on the walls. The walls she had promised herself she would paint, but never got around to it. She would paint soon, Katie promised herself.

Tired from her trip, Katie throws herself on her bed, and dozes off, but sleeps poorly, as she tosses and turns for most of the night.

In the morning, she calls in to work and lets them know she is back and would be coming in to work the following day.

She spends the rest of the day cleaning and getting her place and things back in order. She calls the attorney who took over her cases, they are mostly resolved, he says, and she will not need to take over them.

"Good," Katie says to herself as she hangs up the phone.

Katie calls home to check on her family and lets them know she made it back to L.A. safely. She is glad to turn in early for the night. Katie sleeps restlessly, tossing and turning and waking up often. She will have to get used to her bed all over again. She finally falls asleep late into the night and begins dreaming.

Daniel is there in her dream's vision, walking toward her at the river's edge. He has a sensual look in his eyes, giving her that boyish grin she has loved all of her life. She runs into his arms as they kiss. Suddenly, she hears a distant horrible sound, as she is startled awake. She sits straight up in bed and looks at the alarm clock that reads 6 am. It is time to get up and get dressed for work. She gets out of bed to take a shower. Once dressed for work, she prepares a cup of coffee.

At that moment, the doorbell rings. Katie peeps through the door and sees Travis standing there. She sighs... takes a moment... and then decides to open the door and let him in.

"Travis! What are you doing here so early?"

"Just drove in from a gig in Albuquerque last night. I came straight here, hoping to finally catch you. I've wanted to see you. I've been by many times, and you've never answered your phone."

"I'm sorry, Travis."

"You completely disappeared, Katie. Haven't heard from you in months. I've been worrying about you."

"I really am so sorry, Travis. My father had a stroke, and I've been back home with my parents, and taking care of some legal things."

"I'm sorry to hear that, Katie. How's he doing now? Is everything okay?"

"He's better. Needs to slow down a bit. How have you been?"

"Well, I've been waiting for months for that answer you never gave me."

This is the last thing Katie feels like discussing at the moment. She is confused and still reeling from Daniel's proposal. It seems like a dream now.

"I don't know, Travis. I'm too confused. I'm not sure that we can be all that to each other."

Travis holds her, tries to kiss her.

"I'm not the same, I'm sorry," Katie says to him softly.

"What's different? You still care about me, don't you?" Travis says, hoping for the right answer.

By the look on her face, Travis is not going to get the answer he wants.

"Always. I will always care about you. You're wonderful. But... I think I belong somewhere else, Travis."

A few moments of silence pass. Travis sighs deeply at the realization that he and Katie are not going to be together.

"Well, Katie... Then you need to go and belong."

They hold each other for a few moments, and then she escorts him to the door. He turns back to face her and gives her a kiss on the top of her head and walks out.

Katie closes the door, leans on it, and then closes her eyes. Her mind is somewhere else. Her mind is in Forgotten.

Chapter 22
Henry

"I'm dying!... Somebody help me! I'm dying!"

Henry lies in his bed having one of his usual nightmares. He wakes up screaming in anguish. There is fear written all over his face. He sits up in bed and begins to cry like a small child. Daniel hears his father's scream and comes into his room. Daniel sits by his father on the bed and offers some comfort.

"You're okay, Dad. You were having one of your bad dreams again, that's all. Please calm down."

"I'm fine now, Daniel. Go back to bed."

"It's alright, Dad. I'm up. I have work to do."

Daniel sees his father as a different man now. A man who has been broken, and who has finally been made to pay for the crimes of his family. A man who has had justice served upon him, and a man who has lost his way.

Later that morning Daniel is walking out of the stable as Henry stumbles in. Henry still manages a cane and is holding a near empty bottle of whiskey in the other hand. By the looks of it, he has already had a few.

Henry barks at one of the vaqueros. "Eddie, *trae mi caballo.*"

Eddie hurries off quickly to the stables to get Henry's horse.

"You know what the doctor said about riding with that leg, not to mention the whiskey, Dad!"

"No damn quack tells me what to do, and neither do you, boy!" Henry angrily yells at his son.

Eddie brings Henry's horse over to him. Henry takes another swig from the bottle, drinks until he empties it, and tosses it on the ground.

He struggles onto his horse, as Eddie tries to help him.

"Where are you going, Father," Daniel yells at him, fearing the worse.

"I got something I need to settle once and for all," Henry says and rides off.

Daniel runs into the stable to saddle his horse to go after Henry. He has never seen that look on his father's face, and it frightens him. What is his father up to now?

Henry rides through the fields alone. He is stoic, isolated in the misery which has been his life. As he thinks on it, his entire life. Due to loyalty, his stallion carries him on his back, but seems confused at Henry's erratic behavior in handling him. He rides through the pastures that he has treasured for so long. Land that is now lost forever. As he rides, a look of contempt so evil slowly creeps over his face, a look that no one has witnessed before.

At the Baker farm, George is busy wrangling a few cows into the corral for branding.
George looks better than ever on his horse. His arm has healed and is no longer in a sling. George dismounts. His new farmhand, Nick, is standing there smiling. Nick is the 16-year-old boy that Katie found to work for George. Nick's family had come into some hard times recently, and he was eager to work to help out.

"You ride well, Mr. Baker," Nick says to George.

"I should hope so," George replies. "I've been on a horse since I could walk."

Nick brings over a small calf for George to inspect.

"This one's got some hoof problem," Mr. Baker.

"Please, Nick. Call me, George. Let's get her over to the stall and take a look at it."

As they walk the calf over, "Thanks for the job, Mister... I mean, George. My family can use the money right now. My Dad's been sick, you know."

"Yes, I heard about that. I hope he gets better soon. I'm glad you're here, Nick. I miss having a young man around. Lost my son when he was just about your age."

Nick seems sad to hear this but pleased that George has shared it with him.

"I'll work hard, George," Nick says. "My dad says you've never wanted any help. I'm feeling lucky to have this job."

"Only after school for a couple of hours, and on Saturdays, understand?"

"Yes, sir," Nick says happily.
They smile at one another, and George is feeling some relief that Nick is here to help him with the workload.

"Can't do a man's work anymore, huh, George?"
The peace is broken by Henry's loud voice.

Just then, Henry comes riding up. He is drunk and can hardly keep his mount. George can obviously see that Henry is in bad condition. Nick has a confused look on his face. He has heard the rumors but has never witnessed the men together.

George answers him, "Just like you've had everyone else doing your man's work for you, only—your entire life. What the hell you want, Henry?"

"I came to say..." Henry is having a hard time answering him.

"Well, spit it out and leave."

"I came to say... I'm sorry."

George stands there speechless. He honestly does not know how to respond to Henry. He has never heard Henry say those words in his life. George is uncertain. Should he laugh?

Daisy has heard Henry's arrival and comes out of the house toward them.

"Howdy, Daisy," Henry says, barely able to speak clearly, as intoxicated as he is.

"I came to tell you and George that I'm a no good son of a bitch, and I deserve to rot in hell with my ancestor for all we've done to your family," Henry says taking small breaks between the words.

George and Daisy worry he is about to have a serious accident if he falls off of his horse.

"Let me help you down, Henry," George says to him.

"I'm fine," Henry tries to say with a little pride.

"Listen to him, Henry. For once in your life— please listen to George," Daisy pleads.

Nick just stands there feeling useless and a little scared.

The horse is entirely irritated by now, confused by the way Henry is riding him, and it begins to act up uncontrollably.

Daniel comes riding up behind his father. He takes the reins away from Henry, and dismounts. Daniel has the horse under his control as George helps Henry get off of his horse.

"Please let George drive you home, Henry," Daisy says pleading with him.

"You're drunk, Dad. Please let them get you home," Daniel says to him. "I'm sorry, George. Daisy."

As George and Daniel assist Henry in walking up toward the farmhouse, Henry suddenly collapses and falls to the ground. He grabs his chest, wincing in pain.

"Call for an ambulance, Daisy," George says to her with urgency.

She runs off as Daniel says, "Dad, talk to me."

Henry is not responding, as George says, "Take it easy, Henry. Open your eyes."

Henry slowly opens his eyes and sees Daniel. There is a moment between them, as if asking for forgiveness. Then he looks at George, sending him his usual smirk.

"George..." Henry tries to talk.

"Please Henry, just hang on. Help is on the way."

Daisy comes up with a glass of water, kneels before Henry, and tries to have him drink some, but he is not having any.

"I have more I want to say, George," Henry begins softly.

"Go ahead then."

Struggling with his words Henry says, "I spent my life being evil to you... I've hated what I've done to you for as long as I can remember."

George is so taken aback, but he remains quiet.

Henry continues, "You're the only good man, 'cept my boy here, that I've ever known."

Daniel is emotional and fearing the worst, as Henry continues to talk.

"My grandfather was no good," Henry continues. "And my father I lost. He was a good man like you, George. I've always suspected my grandfather made him disappear. He was going to take me away. He said so many times."

George is deeply saddened to hear this. He had always wondered what had happened to George's father.

"I'm so sorry for you, Henry. I truly am," George says compassionately.

"The day you lost your family, George. That's the day I lost my Pa, too."

George had never heard this. Henry winces in pain and struggles to talk. Daniel holds his father's head in his lap to make him more comfortable. George has never felt sorrier for Henry's struggles as he does now.

"Maybe if my wife would have lived, maybe I could've turned out better. If only I'd had a woman like your Daisy. You're a lucky man, George Baker."

"Thank you for speaking your mind, Henry," George says to him.

"In another lifetime, maybe we could've been friends and gotten along alright," Henry adds.

"Probably so, Henry," George replies kindly.

Daisy comes closer and kneels beside Henry.

"There's something I need to tell you, Henry," Daisy begins.

It is Daisy, so Henry is paying more attention now. He is clearly in pain, but he musters some strength for Daisy.

"You should know... Katie and Patrick are your children, Henry. It happened that night we were together. Although I don't remember it well, and you probably don't, either."

"Daisy... Why didn't you tell me?" Henry struggles to speak. The pain in his eyes is sharper now.

"I'm sorry. You were always so cruel, Henry. I could not bear the thought of you taking the children away from me. You had all the power and money. I didn't want to lose my children. Please forgive me."

The grief on Henry's face is profound. He is sobbing now and regretting every cruel word he ever said about Katie and Patrick. Henry is fully aware this is the precise moment in his life when he has paid for his sins. He has lost the love of children he would never know. He has squandered his own children in return for hatred. If Henry had arrived in hell, this moment was certainly it.

Through heavy tears, Henry begins, "I can't blame you for hating me, Daisy. I'm sure in your heart I didn't deserve your children. I know now that I never did. You loved your kids."

"I'm sorry, Henry." Daisy is sobbing now.

Henry is distraught as he listens to Daisy's sorrowful crying. The only other sounds to be heard are the hill country mourning doves in the treetops of the live oaks. Henry finds himself listening to them now as he lays in Daniel's arms. How odd the doves would be singing just for him today, with their slow drawn out lamenting songs? Like a symphony, the mournful weeping of the doves in harmony with Daisy's crying fill his ears. A few doves take flight, and their wings clatter loudly as they fly closely by. Henry is in tune with every sound, and every noise is sharper and amplified. The breeze scatters among the cattails and calls out to Henry in a way it never has before. Henry wonders to himself now, is this what dying feels like?

Henry still rests in Daniel's arms. He looks up at Daniel and moans and grimaces once again in pain.

"Please, Dad. Stay with me. The ambulance is on the way."

"I've always loved you, son. I know I didn't show it well. I'm sorry I criticized you for your music."

"That's in the past now, Dad."

"You're talented. I'm proud of you, son. Forgive me for being a bad father."

Henry closes his eyes.

"Dad, please stay with me."

Henry opens his eyes again slowly and says to him, "Please take care of Katie, son. Tell her... I'm sorry," and with those last words, Henry's eyes close forever.

Tears stream down Daniel's face. George and Daisy hold one another as she sobs in his arms. The suffering and devastation that was Henry's life is over for him. Henry's agony is over for them all.

Days later, one police car, a hearse, followed by three Champion trucks with their headlights on pass slowly down the road by George and Daisy's farmhouse on the way to Forgotten Cemetery. The sun is low in the horizon as George and Daisy stand on their front porch watching the funeral procession as it passes by.

They are wearing black, as is customary, to attend a funeral. Out of respect for Daniel, George and Daisy will attend.

George sees Daniel as he rides in the first truck, expressionless. He turns to look at them, and they acknowledge each other.

George removes his cowboy hat and places it over his heart, as a symbol of respect. Daniel notices this small gesture. Daisy raises her hand to wave to him, and he sends a polite nod her way.

Daisy and George remain standing until the five vehicles are down the road. George puts his arms around Daisy, puts his hat back on his head, and escorts her to the truck. They drive away from the farm and follow the procession to the cemetery as the sun is setting in the sky.

Chapter 23
Forever Love

The Texas countryside is magnificent as the sun shines brilliantly this cool early December day. The air is crisp, and the fall foliage is almost past peak of color, predictable for late November into early December in the Texas Hill Country. The mesquite trees have turned a pale-yellow color as they spread across the hillsides.

Daniel is riding over the land, reins in, and looks around. Daniel wears a jacket now, as the days have gotten cooler. There is a smoky odor in the air. He looks off into the distance and sees a show of gray smoke as it rises into the sky. He takes off at a gallop to investigate.

Daniel is concerned that some careless individual has started a fire, so he rides his mare fast and hard over the rise.

Finally, Daniel reaches the river and trots his horse over to the river's edge, reins in, looks confused for a moment, and then a huge smile brightens his handsome face.

Katie is standing by the river before a blazing fire she has built in the old stone fireplace. The same old fireplace where her father once retrieved the deed to their land all those many decades ago. Her back is to Daniel as she warms her hands, but then looks over her shoulder and sees him. Daniel rides up close to her and dismounts. He walks over to Katie, still surprised as can be. He is pondering why she is back.

"Hello, Katie," Daniel says standing behind her.

Katie turns to look at him. She is so happy to see him. He looks handsome standing there before her now. Somehow, she knew he would come.

"Hello, Daniel."

"Are your folks okay?"

"They are doing very well. I'm sorry to hear about Henry. Are you okay?"

"Yes. It's been an adjustment not seeing him around the ranch. At any moment, I can imagine him coming out of his office, or expect him to come riding up on horseback at the stables."

"It must be strange to lose someone who has had so much power over everyone. He was definitely a strong presence."

Daniel nods. "The vaqueros don't want to work at the ranch anymore. Most have quit. They claim Henry has left his ghost behind and the ranch is haunted."

"You would think they would feel better not having Henry around?"

Daniel agrees and says, "Henry destroyed so many lives, folks can't believe or accept that he's finally gone."

"You know he was my father?" Katie asks.

"Yes, Daisy and George told me."

"How does that make you feel about... everything?"

"If you're asking if it changes how I feel about you, not at all."

Katie smiles and approaches him.

He is still curious as to why she is in town.

"What brings you back to town, Katie?"

"It's almost the holidays, and I needed to check on my folks."

Daniel feels happy to hear this but was hoping she was in town because of him. Perhaps she had a change of heart. Perhaps she missed him as much as he missed her these months apart.

"This is such a pretty place. Wonderful spot to build a home and raise a family, don't you think?" Katie asks, gazing about and then looking directly into his eyes.

Daniel is surprised by her words. He is praying she is going to stay this time.

"I've always loved you, Daniel."

Daniel's smile says it all. He picks her up into the air and spins her around.

"And I've always known you'd come home to me one day! I love you, Katie Baker!"

Daniel is overwhelmed as he holds her. They tenderly engage in a long kiss.

Back on the Baker's front porch, George and Daisy are in an embrace, and engaging in some kissing of their own. They look out at the peaceful beauty of the land which surrounds them. The immense Texas Hill Country stretches out before them. The land to which

George has devoted his life. The beautiful grazing pastures beyond the hill by the river that his father had loved so dearly had ultimately been returned to its rightful heritage. George was finally home again.

THE END

CPSIA information can be obtained
at www.ICGtesting.com
Printed in the USA
LVHW092017210221
679521LV00007B/912